SPELL Examiner's Manual

PATENT PENDING

Spelling Performance Evaluation for Language and Literacy ™

Julie J. Masterson, PhD · Kenn Apel, PhD · Jan Wasowicz, PhD

With Forewords by Louisa Moats and Shane Templeton

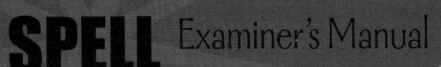

A Prescriptive Assessment of Spelling on CD-ROM

- ◆ Consonants
- ◆ Digraphs
- ◆ Short & Long Vowels
- ◆ Within-Word Doubling
- ◆ Diphthongs & Other Vowels
- ◆ Consonant Clusters

- ◆ Vowel + *r* & Vowel + *l*
- ◆ Silent Consonants
- ◆ Silent *e*
- ◆ Unstressed Vowels
- ◆ Inflections
- ◆ Derivations

LEARNING BY DESIGN, INC.™
Educational Software That Works!™

Grade 2 through Adult

T 51099

SPELL: Spelling Performance Evaluation for Language and Literacy, Learning by Design, Inc., and Educational Software That Works are trademarks of Learning by Design, Inc.

09   08   07   06   05   04   03   02   8   7   6   5   4   3   2   1

ISBN 0-9715133-0-9

Printed in the United States of America

LEARNING BY DESIGN, INC.
Educational Software That Works!™

P.O. Box 5448
Evanston, IL 60604-5448
www.learningbydesign.com

Information and Customer Services

For answers to Frequently Asked Questions about *SPELL*, please visit the Learning By Design, Inc., website at *www.learningbydesign.com*.

Technical Support Information

First, please visit the technical support FAQ page at *www.learningbydesign.com/faqs/index.htm*. If you don't find an answer to your question, please call 1-847-328-8390 between 8 AM and 5 PM CST.

We'd love to hear from you!

Your feedback, comments and suggestions are always welcome. Please contact us by email at *products@learningbydesign.com*.

DIRECTOR® © 1984–2000 Macromedia, Inc. Portions of code © 1995–2001 used under license by Integration New Media, Inc. All other registered trademarks are property of their respective holders.

About the Authors

Dr. Julie J. Masterson is a professor of communication sciences and disorders at Southwest Missouri State University. She has over 20 years of experience working with children who have language problems and language-based learning deficits. Her research interests include phonological intervention, specific spelling disabilities, cognitive abilities in language-learning disabled children, and computer applications. She teaches courses in research design, language-learning disabilities in school-age children and adolescents, language acquisition, and phonology. Dr. Masterson is Vice President of Research and Technology for the American Speech-Language-Hearing Association (ASHA). She is a co-author of Computerized Articulation and Phonology Evaluation System (CAPES; 2001) and serves as a consultant for the development of computer-based products for several corporations. Dr. Masterson is a co-author of *Beyond Baby Talk: From Sounds to Sentences, a Parent's Complete Guide to Language Development*. Dr. Masterson was co-chair of the 1999 annual ASHA convention and served on ASHA's Scientific and Professional Programs Board. She was an associate editor for the *American Journal of Speech-Language Pathology* for five years and has been a guest associate editor for the *Journal of Speech-Language-Hearing Research; Language, Speech, and Hearing Services in Schools*; and *Seminars in Speech and Language*. She served as co-editor for an issue of *Topics in Language Disorders* devoted to spelling assessment and intervention. In addition to her work in speech-language pathology, Dr. Masterson has a degree in elementary education and was a classroom teacher.

Dr. Kenn Apel is a professor and chair of the Department of Communicative Disorders and Sciences at Wichita State University and a fellow of the American Speech-Language-Hearing Association (ASHA). He has over 20 years of experience working with children and adolescents with language problems and language-based learning deficits. Dr. Apel's research interests include specific reading and spelling disabilities in children, adolescents, and adults. He is a former associate editor for *Language, Speech, and Hearing Services in Schools (LSHSS)* and has served as a guest editor for *LSHSS* and *Topics in Language Disorders*. He is a series editor for *Challenges in Language and Literacy*. Dr. Apel served as an area co-coordinator of speech-language pathology and swallowing for the 1999 annual ASHA convention and is a steering committee member for ASHA's Special Interest Division One: Language, Learning, and Education. Dr. Apel is a co-author with Dr. Julie J. Masterson of "Spelling Assessment: Charting a Path to Optimal Intervention," *Topics in Language Disorders* (May, 2000). *SPELL* is based on their work reported in this peer-reviewed publication. Finally, Dr. Apel is a co-author of *Beyond Baby Talk: From Sounds to Sentences, a Parent's Complete Guide to Language Development* (2001).

Dr. Jan Wasowicz is founder, president, and chief learning officer of Learning by Design, Inc. A 20-year veteran of education and technology, Dr. Wasowicz has extensive experience working with children who have speech and language disorders and language-based reading, writing, and spelling problems. She conceived, designed, and developed the original and award-winning Earobics® software products (Cognitive Concepts, Inc., IL; 1997, 1998, 1999). Dr. Wasowicz is the inventor of six software programs for which patents have been awarded or are pending with the U.S. Patent and Trademark Office, including an online early literacy assessment tool funded by the National Institutes of Health. Her teaching experience includes undergraduate- and graduate-level teaching positions at Northwestern University, Elmhurst College, Rush–Presbyterian–St. Luke's Medical Center, and Governors State University. Dr. Wasowicz has co-authored several publications appearing in scientific journals, including the *Journal of the Acoustical Society of America, Perception and Psychophysics, Journal of Phonetics*, and *Journal of Speech and Hearing Research*. Dr. Wasowicz holds a Certificate of Clinical Competence from the American Speech-Language-Hearing Association and a special K–12 teaching certificate from the State Teacher Certification Board of Illinois and is licensed to practice speech-language pathology in the state of Illinois.

Contents

Forewords..ix

Acknowledgments...xi

Part I: Assessment Information

Introduction..3

   Overview of the *SPELL* Program 3

   Description of Spelling 5

   Rationale for *SPELL* 7

   Anticipated Outcomes 8

Administration 9

   General Instructions 9

      Examiner Qualifications 9

      Prerequisite Student Skills 9

      Administration Preparation 9

      Administration Time 9

      Administration Environment 11

      Student Information Form 12

      Assessment Overview 13

      Response Recording and Scoring 14

      Prompting and Feedback Guidelines 15

   Selector Module 15

      Preparation 15

      Procedures 16

      Prompts, Responses, and Feedback 16

      Scoring 16

   Main Test Module 17

      Preparation 17

      Procedures 18

      Prompts, Responses, and Feedback 18

      Cancellation Option...19

Preliminary Analysis Module 19

Additional Test Modules 20

    Preparation 20

    Will-O-Wisp I...20

    Will-O-Wisp II 21

    Magical Pond I 22

    Magical Pond II 22

    Spell Book I 23

    Spell Book II 24

Final Analysis Module 25

Reporting Module 25

    Results Report 25

    Recommendations Report...27

Sharing the Results..30

With Students 30

With Classroom Teachers 30

With Parents 32

Instruction and Remediation 34

General Guidelines...34

Customized Learning Objectives and Related Spelling Activities 36

    Phonological Awareness and Alphabetic Principle 37

    Orthographic Knowledge 38

    Morphological Knowledge and Semantic Relationships 40

    Mental Orthographic Memory 43

    Other Considerations for Spelling Instruction 45

Part II: User Guide

Getting Started with *SPELL* 49

System Requirements 49

    Windows 98/ME 49

    Windows 2000/XP..49

    Macintosh 49

Installation 50

    Windows 50

    Macintosh 50

Set Up 50

    Storing Data 50

    Setting Monitor Resolution 50

    Launching the SPELL Program...50

    Entering a Password..51

    Changing Your Password 51

Main Menu..51

    Test New Student 51

    Resume Testing 55

    Management Tools 58

    Examiner Preview..59

Testing Modules 60

    General Features 60

    Status of Testing in Progress 61

    Student Requires Assistance 63

Administration 64

Sequence 64

Selector Module 64

    Approximate Testing Time..64

    Instructions 65

    Practice Items 65

    Test Items 65

Main Test Module 67

    Approximate Testing Time..67

    Instructions 67

    Practice Items 67

    Test Items 67

Additional Test Modules 69

    Will-O-Wisp I 69

    Will-O-Wisp II 70

    Magical Pond I 72

    Magical Pond II 72

    Spell Book I 74

    Spell Book II 76

Administration Checklist 78

Appendices

Appendix A: Frequently Asked Questions 82

**Appendix B: Suggestions for Implementing Spelling Recommendations
in the Language Arts Curriculum** 88

**Appendix C: Examples and Definitions of Spelling Terms
for Parents and Teachers** 90

Appendix D: Orthographic Spelling Patterns and Rules 92

Appendix E: Morphological Spelling Patterns and Rules 103

Appendix F: Sample Letter to Parents 112

Appendix G: Sample Letter to Teachers 114

Appendix H: List of Selector Module Test Items 116

Appendix I: List of Level 1 Main Test Module Test Items 118

Appendix J: List of Level 2 Main Test Module Test Items 122

Appendix K: List of Level 3 Main Test Module Test Items 128

Appendix L: List of Level 4 Main Test Module Test Items 135

Glossary 143

Helpful Resources 149

  General/Theoretical 149

  Assessment/Intervention 151

References 153

Forewords

Spelling assessment and instruction should be approached as an exercise in language exploration. Through spelling we can learn how well a student processes the speech sound system and how much a student understands about the meaningful parts of words. Spelling can tell a great deal about the student's grasp of our writing system—the orthographic system through which we represent speech. With the *SPELL: Spelling Performance Evaluation for Language and Literacy* assessment system, teachers and specialists can pinpoint exactly what language structures the student needs to understand and can receive expert advice on exactly how to meet those instructional needs.

SPELL embodies the findings of 30 years of research on the structure of English orthography, the developmental stages of learning to spell, and the nature of proficient and deficient spelling. Beginning in about 1970, researchers began to turn away from the traditional view that spelling was a rote, visual memory activity, discovering instead that spelling is one of the most complex forms of language production, mediated by phonological, orthographic, and morphological processing. When the linguistic challenges of spelling were uncovered by research, we could understand more easily why spelling is so difficult for so many students and why people often can read better than they can spell. *SPELL*'s authors have studied the extant literature on these topics and conducted the experiments necessary to produce a theoretically sound and useful tool. They have selected the most valid theories of orthographic learning to organize this instrument and have contributed a valuable innovation to our field.

The study of spelling is the study of words—their history, meaning, grammatical role, and linguistic structure. *SPELL* will direct teachers toward these aspects of language, and encourage the use of more enlightened instructional practices that truly educate students in word study. I am pleased to be among the first to appreciate the excellent work that has gone into this product, and I applaud the authors' achievement.

—Louisa Moats, EdD
Longmont, Colorado

As a subject and as a psychological process, spelling has been radically re-conceptualized over the past quarter century. Spelling knowledge is now understood as being central to learning to read and to write and to the processes of reading and writing. Our understanding of the logic of the English spelling system has been similarly re-conceptualized. We understand that the spelling of words represents information not only at the level of sound but at the level of meaning as well. This coalescence of developmental/psychological research with linguistic analyses of the nature of the spelling system affords some of the most exciting possibilities in contemporary literacy and language assessment and instruction.

Simply put, looking closely at how students spell words offers powerful insight into the nature of their word knowledge and thus the types of information they use when they read and write words. This insight in turn guides appropriate planning and engaging instruction. Until recently, however, there have been few resources that offer guidance to educators and clinicians in applying this strong research base in spelling assessment and instruction. *SPELL: Spelling Performance Evaluation for Language and Literacy* provides this guidance in a focused and effective format. Such a resource is critically important at a time when literacy assessment and instruction are being considered in light of the degree to which they reflect solid research. Perhaps most important, *SPELL* helps educators and clinicians meet the critical challenge of providing effective and appropriate literacy instruction for all learners.

—Shane Templeton, PhD
Foundation Professor of
Curriculum and Instruction
University of Nevada, Reno

Acknowledgments

The authors wish to thank the following individuals for their invaluable contributions to the development of *SPELL*:

- Sue Caspari, MS, CCC-SLP, private practice, Swarthmore, PA

- Kathryn Crider, BA, Southwest Missouri State University, Springfield, MO

- Lyle Hull Davis, MS-Ed, PhD, private practice, Evanston, IL

- Susan Grisko, MS-Ed, private practice, Des Plaines, IL

- Sherry Grobe, BA, private practice, Palatine, IL

- Barbara Hodson, PhD, CCC-SLP, Wichita State University, Wichita, KS

- Terry Hrycyna, MS, CCC-SLP, Lake Bluff School, Shorewood, WI

- Brenda Murphy, BA, MBA, Murphy-Cates Learning Center, Harriman, TN

- Lynn Neils, PhD, CCC-SLP, private practice, Chicago, IL

- Cheryl Scott, PhD, CCC-SLP, Northwestern University, Evanston, IL

- Patricia Scott, MS, CCC-SLP, Springfield Public Schools, Springfield, MO

- Holly A. Shapiro, PhD, CCC-SLP, Ravinia Reading Center, Highland Park, IL

- Anne Whitney, EdD, CCC-SLP, University of Colorado, Boulder, CO

Part I
Assessment Information

Introduction

Overview of the SPELL Program

SPELL: Spelling Performance Evaluation for Language and Literacy is a software assessment tool with 11 modules (see Figure 1) that analyzes a student's patterns of misspelling and provides customized learning objectives for spelling instruction based on the assessment results. The *SPELL* program:

- Administers and scores a student's spelling of preliminary test items **(Selector Module)**

- Determines the most appropriate level of assessment to administer, based on preliminary test item performance **(Selector Module)**

- Collects a spelling sample for analysis **(Main Test Module)**

- Analyzes the student's patterns of misspelling **(Preliminary Analysis Module)**

- Gathers additional information for analysis as needed **(Will-O-Wisp I** and **II, Magical Pond I** and **II,** and **Spell Book I** and **II Modules)**

- Determines the most likely cause or causes of misspelling patterns **(Final Analysis Module)**

- Provides customized learning objectives for spelling instruction **(Reporting Module)**

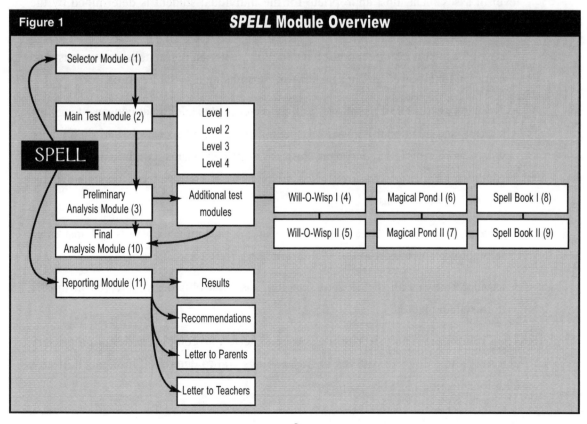

Figure 1 — *SPELL* Module Overview

3

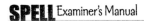

SPELL is designed for administration to students from Grades 2–12 and adults. Administering SPELL to students in Grade 1 will not provide meaningful information. This is because administration of SPELL will likely result in a recommendation for instruction that is no different from the type of instruction that occurs in most first-grade classrooms. However, it is left to the examiner's discretion whether administration to first-grade students might be useful. Administering SPELL to students below the first grade is not recommended, because younger children are not yet expected to have the spelling skills that are measured by SPELL.

The SPELL software assessment tool is designed for individual student administration. SPELL provides a standard format for administration and requires minimal supervision by the examiner. The software presents graphical animations, verbal instructions, and test stimuli to the student, and the individual student then types his or her spelling responses on the keyboard or uses the mouse to respond. The SPELL software then automatically records, scores, and analyzes the student's responses.

The SPELL software assessment tool includes the following 11 modules:

1. The **Selector Module** is used to determine the most appropriate level of the **Main Test Module** to administer to an individual student.

2. The **Main Test Module** is used to collect a sample of the student's spelling of between 82 and 184 words for analysis. There are four levels of the **Main Test Module**, and the level of assessment most appropriate for the individual student is determined by the student's performance during the **Selector Module.**

   - Level 1 assesses common consonant spelling patterns, digraphs, short vowels, and common long-vowel spelling patterns in mostly single-syllable words.

   - Level 2 assesses all of the above spelling patterns plus additional consonant spelling patterns and additional long-vowel spelling patterns, other vowels and diphthongs, within-word doubling, consonant clusters, silent consonants, conditioning and non-conditioning silent *e*, and vowel + *r* and vowel + *l* spelling patterns in single-syllable and multisyllabic words.

   - Level 3 assesses all of the above spelling patterns plus inflected words and unstressed schwa vowels in mostly multisyllabic words.

   - Level 4 assesses all of the above spelling patterns plus derived words in mostly multisyllabic words.

3. The **Preliminary Analysis Module** is used to perform a complex series of proprietary algorithms to recognize patterns of misspellings and to determine how much, if any, additional testing must be completed.

4–9. Six additional test modules—**Will-O-Wisp I** and **II, Magical Pond I** and **II,** and **Spell Book I** and **II**—can be administered, if deemed necessary after the **Main Test Module** data have been analyzed, to obtain information about the student's phoneme and syllable segmentation, phoneme discrimination, base-word spelling, and morphological knowledge skills for the purpose of completing analysis of the student's spelling errors.

10. The **Final Analysis Module** is used to identify the cause or causes of the student's misspellings and to provide customized learning objectives for spelling instruction.

11. The **Reporting Module** is used to preview and print the results of *SPELL*, including performance scores for over 120 common spelling patterns, customized learning objectives for spelling instruction, and letters to parents and teachers.

In addition, several management tools are included in the *SPELL* software (under the **Main Menu)** to help the examiner organize, maintain, and print the student data records. All of these modules and tools are explained in this *Examiner's Manual.* It is recommended that both Part I: Assessment Information and Part II: User Guide be reviewed before administering *SPELL* to students.

Description of Spelling

Spelling is a complex, cognitive-linguistic skill that draws upon several language knowledge domains, including individuals' knowledge of phonology, orthography, morphology and semantic relationships, and learned mental images of words (i.e., mental orthographic images). These language domains contribute to spelling development in important and different ways (e.g., Derwing, Smith, & Wiebe, 1995; Nation & Hulme, 1997; Treiman & Bourassa, 2000).

One area of language knowledge used during spelling is phonological awareness (Masterson & Crede, 1999). Individuals use their phonological awareness skills in spelling by breaking down words into smaller units, such as syllables and phonemes, and then linking these smaller units to their written forms. For individuals who demonstrate difficulties in segmenting words into phonemes, language specialists can predict that spelling will be affected (Nation & Hulme, 1997). In most cases, individuals with poor word segmentation skills will delete letters and/or syllables in the words they spell (e.g., *cat* for *cats, sop* for *stop, relize* for *realize).*

Spelling also requires the ability to discriminate between phonemes (speech sounds) in a meaningful way. For example, a student may not perceive a difference between short vowels *e* and *i* or a student may hear a difference between these two sounds but may not recognize that the difference signals a difference in meaning. When this occurs, a student may spell the two vowel sounds with the same letter.

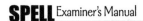

Individuals also must acquire the spelling rules or strategies required to convert spoken language to its written form (Ehri, 2000; Treiman & Bourassa, 2000). An understanding of these strategies, known as orthographic knowledge, includes recognizing the appropriate letters or graphemes that represent different phonemes, and which graphemes or grapheme combinations can occur in different word contexts and positions (e.g., the /k/ sound in *cape* cannot be spelled with a *ck*, because *ck* never spells the /k/ sound in the initial position of a word). Individuals with poor orthographic knowledge are likely to spell words incorrectly, failing to recognize accepted spelling conventions.

Individuals also use knowledge of word meaning, or semantics, to correctly spell words. An understanding of a particular word's meaning helps the student recall the correct spelling of homophones, words that sound the same but have different meanings (e.g., *bare* and *bear*, *dear* and *deer, which* and *witch)*. Individuals who fail to apply their semantic knowledge are likely to confuse the spelling of homophones.

Another important skill that affects spelling is morphological knowledge, which includes the knowledge of semantic relationships between base words and inflected or derived forms (Carlisle, 1995; Fowler & Lieberman, 1995; Treiman, Cassar, & Zukowski, 1994). When an individual is required to spell an unfamiliar word (e.g., *exception),* knowledge of the base form (i.e., *except)* and spelling for certain word endings (i.e., *-ion)* may aid in spelling the unknown word. The student may also draw upon knowledge of rules for modifying base words to correctly spell inflected and derived forms. For example, the morphological rule of dropping a silent *e* at the end of the verb *hope* before adding *-ed* to form the past tense will help the individual correctly spell *hoped*. The need to use morphological knowledge to spell words becomes increasingly important as individuals spell words of greater length and complexity.

Finally, individuals must develop clear mental images of previously read words (e.g., *feet* rather than *fete)*, common syllable structures (e.g., *en-*, as in *enter, engrossed,* and *envelope)*, and word endings (e.g., *-sion* vs. *-tion)*. These mental images, known as mental orthographic images (MOIs), are stored in memory after repeated exposures to them in print (Ehri & Wilce, 1982; Glenn & Hurley, 1993). Clearly developed MOIs allow individuals to quickly recall and spell common, well-known words. Inadequate MOIs, developed due to inappropriate reading strategies, may lead to misspellings when the use of other language knowledge domains is insufficient for correct spelling (e.g., *ubout* for *about* or *buckit* for *bucket)*.

Both children and adults utilize these different language knowledge domains throughout spelling development (Treiman & Bourassa, 2000). The amount that each area contributes to spelling development differs depending on an individual's literacy experiences and the complexity of the words needing to be spelled. Initially, phonological awareness skills play a large role in early spelling development, yet other language domains, such as orthographic knowledge and rudimentary morphological knowledge may also be contributing factors (Treiman & Bourassa, 2000). With additional experiences and learning, spelling development may be positively affected through a deeper understanding and increased use of orthographic, morphological, and semantic knowledge and a larger number of clear mental orthographic images. It is critical, then, to determine how these different knowledge domains affect an individual's spelling abilities (Masterson & Apel, 2000).

Rationale for *SPELL*

In recent years, considerable empirical and theoretical advances in the understanding of literacy development have occurred. Along with these advances, the need for measurement tools that accurately describe an individual's literacy skills has emerged. Without a well-designed, theoretically grounded method for determining the current level of an individual's literacy capabilities, educators run the risk of providing less-than-effective instructional or remedial programs. *SPELL: Spelling Performance Evaluation for Language and Literacy* was developed to address this need for an accurate measurement tool in one area of literacy development— spelling—and to provide specific and optimally constructed learning objectives based on an individual's current spelling abilities.

SPELL was designed to determine which of the critical knowledge language domains an individual is and is not using when spelling. Recall that these domains include phonological awareness, orthographic knowledge, morphological knowledge (including semantic relationships), and mental orthographic memory.

Other spelling assessments determine the percentage of correctly spelled words out of a total set of words. From this quantitative score, the student's spelling level is determined. However, knowing the ratio of correctly spelled words to misspelled words or spelling grade level does not provide the specialist with direction for instruction or remediation (Masterson & Apel, 2000). *SPELL* goes a step further by helping educators determine which language knowledge domains the speller is and is not using, thus allowing educators to optimally tailor instruction or remediation to the individual based on the customized learning objectives provided by *SPELL*.

Using carefully constructed spelling lists that represent specific types of spelling knowledge used throughout the spelling-acquisition process, *SPELL* analyzes an individual's responses for patterns of errors and then determines factors that may contribute to the identified error patterns. These factors include the language knowledge domains discussed above that have been found to contribute to spelling development and spelling disorders; namely phonological awareness, orthographic knowledge, semantic knowledge, morphological

7

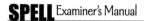

knowledge, and mental orthographic memory. Once the influential factors have been identified, *SPELL* provides customized learning objectives for individualized instruction or remediation to improve the individual's spelling. Thus, unlike other spelling assessment tools, *SPELL* provides systematic and valuable instructional and remedial information based on what is now known about spelling development.

Anticipated Outcomes

Use of *SPELL* enables specialists to determine possible contributing factors for an individual's spelling errors and then to develop a systematic plan for instruction or remediation of spelling using the customized learning objectives provided. *SPELL*'s logical and theoretically grounded approach to spelling assessment will aid educators in determining how best to help an individual improve his or her spelling skills, as well as to document progress in spelling acquisition. A thorough understanding of spelling development coupled with a comprehensive tool to assess an individual's spelling capabilities (and the language knowledge domains contributing to those abilities) is crucial to developing appropriate and effective spelling-development programs.

This time-saving tool automatically collects, analyzes, and scores the student's responses, writes reports and goals for the individual student, and creates letter-style reports so the specialist can easily share results with parents and classroom teachers. With *SPELL*'s assistance in developing the most appropriate intervention plan, the specialist has the specific direction needed to confidently proceed with implementing the most efficient and cost-effective spelling instruction program for the individual student.

Administration

General Instructions

Examiner Qualifications

SPELL is intended for use by certified and licensed professionals. The software assessment program can also be administered by teacher aides and other support personnel because *SPELL* does not require professional training in test administration, scoring, and interpretation. However, *SPELL* should be administered under the specific guidelines provided in this manual.

Prerequisite Student Skills

SPELL is appropriate for use by students whose developmental age is 7 years and above. Students should have general familiarity with using a computer keyboard and a mouse and have adequate ability to follow oral directions.

Administration Preparation

It is strongly recommended that the examiner take adequate time to become familiar with the *SPELL* program prior to administering *SPELL* to a student. A careful review of both parts of the *Examiner's Manual* and a complete preview of the *SPELL* software itself prior to administering *SPELL* will ensure meaningful results and will maximize the benefits of using the *SPELL* software. If questions remain after reviewing the *Examiner's Manual*, see the *Frequently Asked Questions* page in Appendix A. The *Examiner Preview* feature can be accessed from the **Main Menu** and provides the opportunity for the examiner (and the student) to preview the instructions and practice items for the **Selector Module** and **Main Test Module** and for each of the six additional test modules. The examiner can also preview an optional reward animation from the *Examiner Preview* screen.

SPELL should be administered to an individual student at a computer workstation. Check and adjust the audio volume prior to administration. This is particularly important if *SPELL* is being administered with headphones (which is highly recommended), as it will be difficult to check and adjust the volume without interruption once the student begins the assessment.

Administration Time

SPELL is an untimed assessment tool. One of the tool's strengths is its ability to individualize the components administered based on the profile exhibited by the student. Consequently, administration time varies from student to student. Completion of the **Selector Module** and **Main Test Module** of *SPELL* takes approximately 30–60 minutes, depending on the student's own pace and the level (i.e., the number of words) being tested (see Table 1). Completion of the additional test modules, if required, takes an additional 10–15 minutes, depending on how

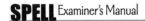

many modules are administered and how many test items are administered in each module. The administration of the additional test modules and the number of test items administered in each module are determined by the individual student's performance on the **Main Test Module.**

Tables 1 and 2 provide average testing times and recommended guidelines for administration of the *SPELL* modules. As with any test administration, it is incumbent upon the examiner to monitor the student's level of attention and fatigue, and to provide breaks in testing as needed. Because *SPELL* features automatic bookmarking—keeping track of where the student last exited the program and automatically returning the student to that same point in the program when the student resumes testing—the examiner can easily allow the student a break at any time during administration of the *SPELL* test.

Average Test Administration Times and Recommended Schedule for Main Test Module

Table 1

Level	Number of Words	Average Testing Time	Recommended Schedule
1	82	30–40 min.	**Three 15-minute sessions** Schedule each session on a different day, allowing 2–3 days between sessions, if possible.
2	141	35–45 min.	**Three 15-minute sessions** Schedule each session on a different day, allowing 2–3 days between sessions, if possible.
3	179	45–60 min.	**Three 20-minute sessions** Schedule each session on a different day, allowing 2–3 days between sessions, if possible.
4	184	45–60 min.	**Three 20-minute sessions** Schedule each session on a different day, allowing 2–3 days between sessions, if possible.

Average Test Administration Times and Recommended Schedule for Additional Test Modules

Table 2

Additional Test Module	Average Testing Time	Recommended Schedule
Will-O-Wisp I	3–5 min.	**Single session** May complete testing across more than one session, if desired.
Will-O-Wisp II	3–5 min.	**Single session** May complete testing across more than one session, if desired.
Magical Pond I	3–5 min.	**Single session** May complete testing across more than one session, if desired.
Magical Pond II	3–12 min.	**Single session** May complete testing across more than one session, if desired.
Spell Book I	3–12 min.	**Single session** May complete testing across more than one session, if desired.
Spell Book II	3–12 min.	**Single session** May complete testing across more than one session, if desired.

Administration Environment

As in any testing situation, the physical and emotional environment should be reasonably comfortable and free from distraction. It is essential that the testing location is quiet. Use of quality headphones during administration is highly recommended. Lighting must be appropriate and must not create glare on the computer screen.

To establish rapport, it is recommended that the examiner engage the student in a few moments of conversation prior to starting the test. During administration of the practice items (in the **Selector Module** and additional test modules only), the examiner should be seated next to the student. As with any test, the validity of the assessment results is determined by the student's level of cooperation and effort to respond as best as he or she can. For this reason, the examiner should visually monitor the student throughout the administration of *SPELL* to

11

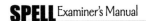

ensure that the student is successfully engaged with the assessment. It is left to the examiner's discretion whether to remain seated with the student throughout the administration of the test items or to monitor periodically as the student completes the test items.

Student Information Form

Prior to administering *SPELL*, the examiner completes a Student Information Form for the student. The Student Information Form is accessed from the ***Main Menu*** by selecting *Test New Student*. Completion of this form creates a record of a student's information, including name, gender, date of birth, age, and grade. The examiner also records his or her name, the name of the school or clinic where the testing is conducted, and the date of testing. The student's chronological age at time of testing is automatically computed by *SPELL*. If the student completed a quantitative spelling test—for example, the Test of Written Spelling–4 (TWS–4) (Larsen, Hammill, & Moats, 1999), within six months prior to the date of the *SPELL* assessment, the spelling grade-level score from that test may be entered (this is optional) to help determine the most appropriate beginning test item for the *SPELL* **Selector Module.**

When completing the Student Information Form, the examiner also selects which character will narrate and guide the student through *SPELL*. The fairy, Fiona, is recommended for students in Grade 3 and below. The wizard, Quinn, is recommended for students in Grades 4–12 and adults. If neither guide is selected, the *SPELL* program automatically selects a guide based on the student's grade as entered on the Student Information Form.

The examiner also selects whether the student will receive reward animations during administration of *SPELL*. The animations are presented in a story format that unfolds between groups of test items to give the student brief, periodic breaks and to help keep the student motivated and on task. The reward animations add approximately 6 minutes to the total administration time and are recommended for all students—including adults, who also enjoy seeing the animations. However, presentation of the reward animations is left to the examiner's discretion.

Information entered on the Student Information Form is displayed onscreen when the student begins and completes a test module and is included in the reports provided by the **Reporting Module.**

Student Information

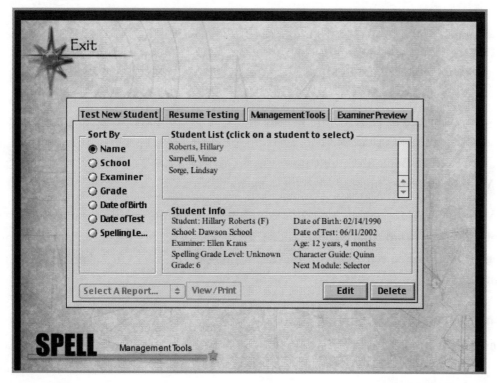

Assessment Overview

Administration of *SPELL* begins with the **Selector Module.** The student is instructed to spell words that are presented verbally. Administration begins with three practice items. Then the test items are presented until a basal and a ceiling are established or until sufficient data are obtained to determine the appropriate level of assessment to administer in the **Main Test Module.** When this occurs, the *SPELL* program automatically discontinues the **Selector Module** and presents the instructions for the **Main Test Module.** (At this time, the student could take a break if the examiner wishes, but he or she is not required to do so by the program.)

The *SPELL* program then continues with automatic selection of the assessment level and administration of the **Main Test Module.** The student is instructed to spell words that are presented verbally. In the unlikely event that the **Selector Module** placed the student in a level of assessment that is too high, the **Main Test Module** will automatically and seamlessly adjust the assessment level and will complete testing at a more appropriate level.

Once the **Main Test Module** is completed, the **Preliminary Analysis Module** analyzes the student's misspellings from the **Main Test Module** and determines whether information about the student's phoneme and syllable segmentation, phoneme discrimination, base-word spelling, and morphological knowledge skills is needed to complete analysis of the spelling errors. The student may take a break during the **Preliminary Analysis Module** as the computer

13

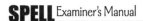

performs the analysis of the data collected in the **Main Test Module,** but he or she is not required to do so by the program. After this analysis, the student may receive additional testing with one or more of the six additional test modules. The two **Will-O-Wisp Modules** probe the student's segmentation of misspelled words into phonemes and misspelled words into syllables. The two **Magical Pond Modules** probe the student's phonemic discrimination of misspelled vowels and liquids. The two **Spell Book Modules** probe the student's spelling of base words that correspond to inflected and derived word forms presented in the **Main Test Module** and probe the student's understanding and use of morphological knowledge for spelling. The **Spell Book Modules** are presented only when Level 3 or Level 4 of the **Main Test Module** has been administered to the student.

When the *SPELL* program has gathered all the required information, the analyses are completed in the **Final Analysis Module.** The student's spelling performance scores and customized learning objectives for spelling instruction can be previewed and printed using the **Reporting Module.**

Response Recording and Scoring

Selector Module

During administration of the **Selector Module,** the student types in each spelling response using the keyboard and then uses a mouse to click **OK.** The computer then records and scores each response as correct or incorrect to determine the most appropriate level of assessment to administer in the **Main Test Module.** Administration of the **Selector Module** is automatically stopped once a basal and a ceiling have been established or once sufficient data are obtained to determine the appropriate level of assessment to administer in the **Main Test Module.**

Main Test Module

During administration of the **Main Test Module,** the student types in each spelling response using the keyboard and then uses a mouse to click **OK.** Once the student has completed the first 20 items of the **Main Test Module,** the student's recorded responses for selected spelling patterns within the first 20 items are scored by the computer to determine if the student was correctly placed in the most appropriate level of assessment. In the unlikely event that the **Selector Module** placed the student in a level of assessment that is too high, the *SPELL* program will automatically and seamlessly adjust the assessment level and will complete testing at a more appropriate level. All test items in the finally selected assessment level are administered to the student at this time.

Preliminary Analysis Module

Upon completion of the **Main Test Module,** the student's responses are analyzed. The analysis is based on a complex series of proprietary algorithms, which recognize patterns of misspellings and consequently form hypotheses about the sources of misspelling and determine how much, if any, additional testing must be completed.

Additional Test Modules

The student's responses during administration of the six additional test modules—**Will-O-Wisp I** and **II, Magical Pond I** and **II,** and **Spellbook I** and **II**—are entered by mouseclick or by keyboard and mouseclick and recorded by the computer. The responses collected by the additional test modules are sent to the **Final Analysis Module** and analyzed together with the responses collected by the **Main Test Module** to identify the cause or causes of the student's misspellings.

Final Analysis Module

The **Final Analysis Module** further analyzes responses collected by the **Main Test Module,** together with responses collected by any additional test modules. The analysis confirms or modifies the initial hypotheses formulated in the **Preliminary Analysis Module,** identifies the cause or causes of the student's misspellings, and provides customized learning objectives for spelling instruction.

Prompting and Feedback Guidelines

As with any other assessment tool, the validity of the *SPELL* analyses and recommendations is compromised if prompts other than those provided by the *SPELL* program are provided to the student. General feedback and reward animations are provided by *SPELL* during the test to help keep the student focused and on task. It is left to the examiner's discretion whether to provide additional general encouragement (e.g., comments to keep the student motivated and on task) during test administration. During presentation of the practice items, the student may request as many repetitions of the verbal stimulus as desired. However, during presentation of the test items, if a student's response on a particular test item is delayed, or if the student requests it, the program will provide only a single repetition of the verbal stimulus. The examiner should not deviate from this format by repeating test items for the student. The next section describes each module in detail.

Selector Module

Administration of the *SPELL* program always begins with the **Selector Module.** This module is used to determine the most appropriate level of the **Main Test Module** to administer to an individual student.

Preparation

When the Prepare to Begin Test screen is displayed, the examiner prepares the student for the assessment by comfortably situating him or her in front of the computer. If the student is using headphones (which is highly recommended), the examiner checks that the headphones are comfortably in place and that the volume is appropriate. The student or the examiner then uses a mouse to click **OK** to begin the assessment.

Procedures

Fiona (the fairy) or Quinn (the wizard) greets the student, explains the purpose of the task, and guides the student through the **Selector Module.** The **Selector Module** presents three practice items (at which time it is recommended that the examiner sit with the student) and a maximum of 40 test items. The starting test item is automatically determined by the student's grade or spelling grade level as entered on the Student Information Form. Administration of the **Selector Module** continues until a sufficient number of test items have been presented to determine which level of assessment to subsequently administer in the **Main Test Module.**

Prompts, Responses, and Feedback

The character guide—either Fiona or Quinn—prompts the student to spell a word by requesting the student's attention and then presenting the target word in isolation, in a sentence, and again in isolation (e.g., "Listen…. Cat. The cat chased the mouse. Cat"). If the student does not respond within 10 seconds, the computer will repeat the verbal stimulus presentation one time. The student may also request replay of the verbal stimulus by clicking **Repeat.** There is no limit on the number of requested repetitions of the verbal stimulus allowed for the practice items. For the test items, only one repetition is allowed. The student types his or her spelling response on the keyboard, with simultaneous display of the typed response onscreen, and then uses a mouse to click **OK** to proceed to the next item. Corrective feedback from the character guide is provided for the practice items. No corrective feedback is provided for the test items. The examiner is allowed to assist the student during the administration of the practice items and is encouraged to sit next to the student while these items are administered. No assistance is allowed during administration of the test items. If the reward animations are turned on, a graphical animation is presented to reward the student for completion of the **Selector Module.** The character guide will let the student know when the first part of the test (i.e., the **Selector Module**) has been completed.

Scoring

The student's spelling responses are automatically scored as either correct or incorrect by *SPELL* and presentation of test items continues until a basal (4 correct out of 6 consecutive responses) and a ceiling (3 consecutive errors or less than 70% correct in a set of 10 words) are established. The level at which the student reached a ceiling determines the level of assessment that will be administered in the **Main Test Module.** If no ceiling is established, the highest level (Level 4) of **Main Test Module** is subsequently administered. If no basal is established, the lowest level (Level 1) of the **Main Test Module** is subsequently administered. *SPELL* automatically discontinues administration of the **Selector Module** when a sufficient number of test items have been presented, and it automatically continues with administration of the **Main Test Module** by presenting the instructions for the **Main Test Module.** If the student requires a break, or if a break in testing is desired due to administration requirements, the examiner may suspend testing at the end of the **Selector Module** and then later resume testing at the beginning of the **Main Test Module.**

Selector Module Test Item

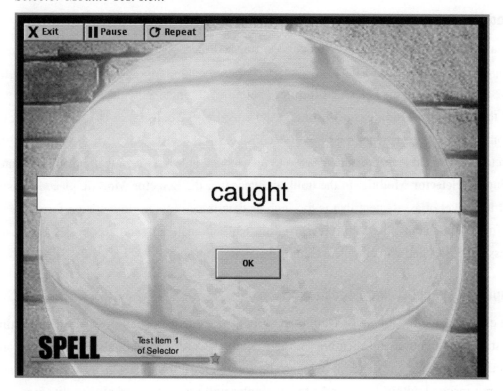

Main Test Module

The **Main Test Module** is used to collect a sample of the student's spelling of between 82 and 184 words. Upon completion of the **Selector Module**, *SPELL* automatically determines the most appropriate level of assessment for the individual student and continues with administration of the **Main Test Module** at that level of assessment. Some test items in the **Main Test Module** may have already been presented during administration of the **Selector Module.** If so, these words are not presented again and the student's spelling of these items in the **Selector Module** is automatically transferred to the **Main Test Module.**

Preparation

If continuing directly from the **Selector Module,** no preparation is needed. If the student exited the program after completion of the **Selector Module** and is returning to complete the **Main Test Module,** the program is ready to administer the **Main Test Module** when the

Prepare to Resume Test screen is displayed. The examiner checks that the student is ready to continue testing. If the student is using headphones (which is highly recommended), the examiner checks that the headphones are comfortably in place and that the volume is appropriate. The student or the examiner then uses a mouse to click **OK** to begin the **Main Test Module.**

Procedures

Fiona or Quinn explains that the student has finished the first part of the test and will now complete the second part of the test. The task requirements in this section of the test are the same as they were in the **Selector Module.** Therefore, no practice items are presented. Level 1 of the **Main Test Module** consists of 82 test items; Level 2 consists of 141 test items; Level 3 consists of 179 test items; and Level 4 consists of 184 test items. All test items in the selected assessment level are administered to the student, unless an item was already presented during the **Selector Module.** In the unlikely event that the **Selector Module** placed the student in a level of assessment that is too high as determined by the student's performance on the first 20 test items, the **Main Test Module** will automatically and seamlessly adjust the assessment level and will complete testing at a more appropriate level.

Prompts, Responses, and Feedback

The character guide—Fiona or Quinn—prompts the student to spell a word by requesting the student's attention and then presenting the target word in isolation, in a sentence, and again in isolation (e.g., "Listen…. Chain. The chain fell off my bike. Chain"). If the student does not respond within 10 seconds, the computer will repeat the verbal stimulus presentation one time. The student may also request replay of the verbal stimulus by clicking **Repeat.** Only one repetition is allowed for the test items. The student types his or her spelling response on the keyboard, with simultaneous display of the typed response onscreen, and then uses a mouse to click **OK** to confirm the spelling and to proceed to the next item. No assistance is allowed during administration of the test items. If the examiner has left them on, reward animations are periodically presented throughout the **Main Test Module** to keep the student motivated and on task. If the reward animations are turned on, a graphical animation is presented to reward the student for completion of the **Main Test Module.** The character guide lets the student know when the second part of the test (i.e., the **Main Test Module)** has been completed.

Main Test Module Test Item

Cancellation Option

After the student has finished spelling the first 20 words of the **Main Test Module,** *SPELL* automatically checks for a minimum spelling accuracy level for selected spelling patterns. If the student does not meet the minimal criterion set by the program, *SPELL* will automatically and seamlessly drop to the next lowest level of the **Main Test Module.** If the student does not meet the minimal criterion set by *SPELL* for the first 20 items of Level 1, the program will pause to alert the examiner that the student may not have minimal spelling proficiency and that the *SPELL* assessment tool may not be appropriate for this student. At this point, the examiner has the option to continue or to cancel testing for the student.

Preliminary Analysis Module

The **Preliminary Analysis Module** is used to perform a complex series of proprietary algorithms to recognize patterns of misspellings; to form hypotheses about the sources of misspellings; and to determine how much, if any, additional testing must be completed.

Additional Test Modules

Six additional test modules—**Will-O-Wisp I** and **II, Magical Pond I** and **II,** and **Spell Book I** and **II**—are administered only as needed to obtain information about the student's phoneme and syllable segmentation, phoneme discrimination, base-word spelling, and morphological knowledge skills to complete analysis of the student's spelling errors in the **Main Test Module.** *SPELL* is not designed to evaluate any of the above-listed skills in isolation and should not be used to do so. The specific test items presented to an individual student during the additional test modules are determined solely by that student's spelling performance in the **Main Test Module.** The responses collected by the additional test modules are evaluated with respect to that student's specific spelling errors. Used in isolation, the additional test modules may not provide a valid assessment of a student's skills. Consequently, it is not possible to directly access any of the additional test modules.

Administration of the additional test modules, the number of test items administered, and the specific items presented in each module are determined by the individual student's performance on the **Main Test Module.** Like the **Selector** and **Main Test Modules,** the additional test modules can be administered in more than one session, as necessary.

Preparation

When the Prepare to Resume Test screen is displayed, the examiner prepares the student by comfortably situating him or her in front of the computer. If the student is using headphones (which is highly recommended), the examiner checks that the headphones are comfortably in place and that the volume is appropriate. The student or the examiner then uses a mouse to click **OK** to begin the additional testing.

Will-O-Wisp I

Procedures

Fiona or Quinn guides the student to the setting for **Will-O-Wisp I.** This module consists of five practice items followed by presentation of test items that probe the student's ability to segment phonemes specific to the types of misspellings exhibited by the student in the **Main Test Module.** Administration of the **Will-O-Wisp I Module** continues until a sufficient number of test items have been presented to evaluate each of the student's identified patterns of misspelling.

Prompts, Responses, and Feedback

The Will-O-Wisp requests the student's attention and prompts the student to click on him (represented by the magical orb) once for each sound he or she hears in a given word. If the student does not respond within 10 seconds, the computer will repeat the verbal stimulus presentation one time. The student may also request replay of the verbal stimulus by clicking **Repeat.** There is no limit on the number of requested repetitions of the verbal stimulus allowed for the practice items. For the test items, only one repetition is allowed. The student makes his or her response by clicking on the orb once for each sound in a word and then clicking on the water when finished. Corrective feedback from the Will-O-Wisp is provided for the practice items. No corrective feedback is provided for the test items. The examiner is allowed to assist the student during the administration of the practice items and is encouraged to sit next to the student while these items are administered. No assistance is allowed during administration of the test items. An animation is presented to signal the completion of the **Will-O-Wisp I Module.**

Scoring

The student's responses are automatically scored as either correct or incorrect by the software program. These data, combined with other performance data, are used by the **Final Analysis Module** to help interpret the student's patterns of misspellings and are not made available to the examiner.

Will-O-Wisp II

Procedures

Fiona or Quinn guides the student to the setting for **Will-O-Wisp II.** This module consists of three practice items followed by presentation of test items that probe the student's ability to segment syllables specific to the types of misspellings exhibited by the student in the **Main Test Module.** Administration of the **Will-O-Wisp II Module** continues until a sufficient number of test items have been presented to evaluate each of the student's identified patterns of misspelling.

Prompts, Responses, and Feedback

The Will-O-Wisp requests the student's attention and prompts the student to click on him (represented by the magical orb) once for each syllable he or she hears in a given word. If the student does not respond within 10 seconds, the computer will repeat the verbal stimulus presentation one time. The student may also request replay of the verbal stimulus by clicking **Repeat.** There is no limit on the number of requested repetitions of the verbal stimulus allowed for the practice items. For the test items, only one repetition is allowed. The student makes his or her response by clicking on the orb once for each syllable in the word and then clicking anywhere on the water when finished. Corrective feedback from the Will-O-Wisp is provided for the practice items. No corrective feedback is provided for the test items. The examiner is allowed to assist the student during the administration of the practice items and is encouraged to sit next to the student while these items are administered. No assistance is allowed during administration of the test items. An animation is presented to signal the completion of the **Will-O-Wisp II Module.**

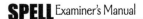

Scoring

The student's responses are automatically scored as either correct or incorrect by the software program. These data, combined with other performance data, are used by the **Final Analysis Module** to help interpret the student's patterns of misspellings and are not made available to the examiner.

Magical Pond I

Procedures

Fiona or Quinn guides the student to the setting for **Magical Pond I.** This module consists of four practice items followed by presentation of test items that probe the student's ability to phonemically discriminate between vowels specific to the types of misspellings exhibited by the student in the **Main Test Module.** Administration of the **Magical Pond I Module** continues until a sufficient number of test items have been presented to evaluate each of the student's identified patterns of misspelling.

Prompts, Responses, and Feedback

The Will-O-Wisp requests the student's attention and prompts the student to listen as a word is repeated over and over and to click on him (represented by the magical orb) when he or she hears a different word (e.g., "back-back-back-back-back-back-bake"). The student makes his or her response by clicking on the orb when he or she hears a different word (i.e., *bake)*. Unlike the other modules, neither **Magical Pond Module** allows students to have the practice or test items repeated. Corrective feedback from the Will-O-Wisp is provided for the practice items. No corrective feedback is provided for the test items. The examiner is allowed to assist the student during the administration of the practice items and is encouraged to sit next to the student while these items are administered. No assistance is allowed during administration of the test items. An animation is presented to signal the completion of the **Magical Pond I Module.**

Scoring

The student's responses are automatically scored as either correct or incorrect by the software program. These data, combined with other performance data, are used by the **Final Analysis Module** to help interpret the student's patterns of misspellings and are not made available to the examiner.

Magical Pond II

Procedures

Fiona or Quinn guides the student to the setting for **Magical Pond II.** This module consists of four practice items followed by presentation of test items that probe the student's ability to phonemically discriminate liquid and vowel phonemes specific to the types of misspellings exhibited by the student in the **Main Test Module.** Administration of the **Magical Pond II Module** continues until a sufficient number of test items have been presented to evaluate each of the student's identified patterns of misspelling.

Prompts, Responses, and Feedback

The Will-O-Wisp requests the student's attention and prompts the student to listen as a word is repeated over and over and to click on him (represented by the magical orb) when he or she hears a different word (e.g., "fur-fur-fur-fur-fur-fuh"). The student makes his or her response by clicking on the orb when he or she hears a different word (i.e., *fuh)*. Unlike the other modules, neither **Magical Pond Module** allows students to have the practice or test items repeated. Corrective feedback from the Will-O-Wisp is provided for the practice items. No corrective feedback is provided for the test items. The examiner is allowed to assist the student during the administration of the practice items and is encouraged to sit next to the student while these items are administered. No assistance is allowed during administration of the test items. An animation is presented to signal the completion of the **Magical Pond II Module.**

Scoring

The student's responses are automatically scored as either correct or incorrect by the software program. These data, combined with other performance data, are used by the **Final Analysis Module** to help interpret the student's patterns of misspellings and are not made available to the examiner.

Spell Book I

Procedures

Fiona or Quinn guides the student to the setting for **Spell Book I.** This module consists of three practice items followed by presentation of test items that probe the student's ability to spell base words specific to the misspellings of inflected and derived words exhibited by the student in the **Main Test Module** of Level 3 and Level 4. This information, combined with other performance data collected, is used to determine whether the student has knowledge of base-word spelling to assist with spelling inflected and derived forms of words. Administration of the **Spell Book I Module** continues until a sufficient number of test items have been presented to evaluate each of the student's identified patterns of misspelling.

Prompts, Responses, and Feedback

Fiona or Quinn requests the student's attention and prompts the student to spell a word presented in isolation, in a sentence, and again in isolation (e.g., "Listen.... Desk. A student sits at a desk. Desk"). If the student does not respond within 10 seconds, the computer will repeat the verbal stimulus presentation one time. The student may also request replay of the verbal stimulus by clicking **Repeat.** There is no limit on the number of requested repetitions of the verbal

stimulus allowed for the practice items. For the test items, only one repetition is allowed. The student types his or her spelling response on the keyboard, with simultaneous display of the typed response onscreen, and then uses a mouse to click **OK** to proceed to the next item. Corrective feedback from the character guide is provided for the practice items. No corrective feedback is provided for the test items. The examiner is allowed to assist the student during the administration of the practice items and is encouraged to sit next to the student while these items are administered. No assistance is allowed during administration of the test items. The character guide reappears to signal the completion of the **Spell Book I Module.**

Scoring

The student's responses are automatically scored as either correct or incorrect by the software program. These data, combined with other performance data, are used by the **Final Analysis Module** to help interpret the student's patterns of misspellings and are not made available to the examiner.

Spell Book II

Procedures

Fiona or Quinn guides the student to the setting for **Spell Book II.** This module consists of three practice items followed by presentation of test items that probe the student's morphological knowledge of the relationship between base words and their inflected and derived forms specific to the types of misspellings exhibited by the student in the **Main Test Module** of Level 3 and Level 4. Administration of the **Spell Book II Module** continues until a sufficient number of test items have been presented to evaluate each of the student's identified patterns of misspelling.

Prompts, Responses, and Feedback

Fiona or Quinn requests the student's attention and prompts the student to complete a sentence by typing a word that is related to a word presented before the sentence (e.g., "Listen.... Musician. He likes to play _____"). If the student does not respond within 10 seconds, the computer will repeat the verbal stimulus presentation one time. The student may also request replay of the verbal stimulus by clicking **Repeat.** There is no limit on the number of requested repetitions of the verbal stimulus allowed for the practice items. For the test items, only one repetition is allowed. The student types his or her spelling response on the keyboard, with simultaneous display of the typed response onscreen, and then uses a mouse to click **OK** to proceed to the next item. Corrective feedback from the character guide is provided for the practice items. No corrective feedback is provided for the test items. The examiner is allowed to assist the student during the administration of the practice items and is encouraged to sit next to the student while these items are administered. No assistance is allowed during administration of the test items. A graphical animation is presented to signal the completion of the **Spell Book II Module.**

Scoring

The student's responses are automatically scored as either correct or incorrect by the software program. Because this task assesses the student's knowledge of the relationship between base words and inflected or derived forms, the *SPELL* program uses its artificial intelligence to determine the student's intended response, even if the student's response was incorrectly spelled. For example, if the student types in "majic" when asked to complete the sentence "Magician. A magician performs _____," this response will be scored as correct because the *SPELL* program is able to determine that the student's intended response was "magic." **Note:** This scoring logic allows *SPELL* to determine if the student has an understanding of the relationship between base words and inflected or derived forms, even though the student may not correctly spell a particular base word. The data collected by the **Spell Book II Module,** combined with other performance data, are used by the **Final Analysis Module** to help interpret the student's patterns of misspellings and are not made available to the examiner.

Final Analysis Module

The **Final Analysis Module** further analyzes responses collected by the **Main Test Module,** together with responses collected by any additional test modules to confirm or modify the initial hypotheses formulated in the **Preliminary Analysis Module,** to identify the cause or causes of the student's misspellings, and to provide customized learning objectives for spelling instruction. When the **Final Analysis Module** has completed its analysis, the *SPELL* assessment tool alerts the examiner that the program is finished. The examiner can then preview and print the results of *SPELL* at that time.

Reporting Module

SPELL allows previewing and printing of the results of the student's assessment, including performance scores for over 120 common spelling patterns, customized learning objectives for spelling instruction, and letter-style reports for parents and teachers. The examiner may wish to refer to the Glossary for an explanation of terms that appear in the reports. The **Reporting Module** is accessed through the *Management Tools* folder tab.

Results Report

The examiner can preview and print the *SPELL* Results Report. This report shows the individual student's spelling performance scores.

Sample Results Report

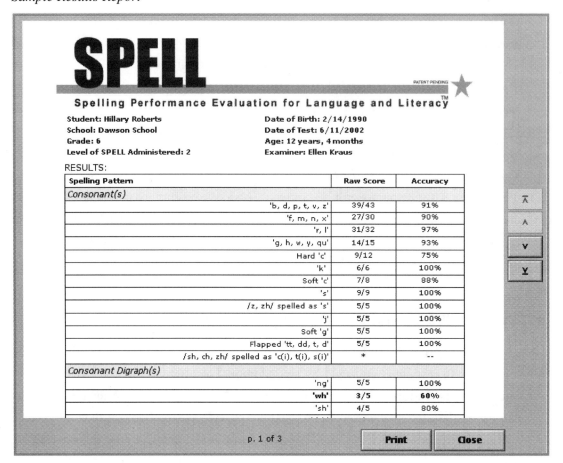

Student Information

The student's identifying information, as entered by the examiner in the Student Information Form, and the level of *SPELL* administered to the individual student is displayed at the top of the *SPELL* Results Report.

Scores

The Results Report contains the raw score and spelling performance accuracy score for each spelling pattern assessed in the level of *SPELL* that was administered to the individual student. Spelling patterns for which the student achieved accuracy of 60% or below are highlighted in bold font on the *SPELL* Results Report. These patterns are considered potential target patterns for instruction or remediation. Recommendations for direct spelling instruction for each of these potential target patterns are available in the Recommendations Report. Patterns for which the student scored above 60% and below 100% are considered to be emerging. The student may not benefit from direct instruction on these spelling patterns at the single-word level. However, see "Other Considerations for Spelling Instruction" (page 45) for suggestions about how to encourage further development of those spelling patterns for which a student scores above 60% and below 100%.

Recommendations Report

The examiner can preview and print the *SPELL* Recommendations Report. This report lists the recommendations for spelling instruction.

Sample Recommendations Report

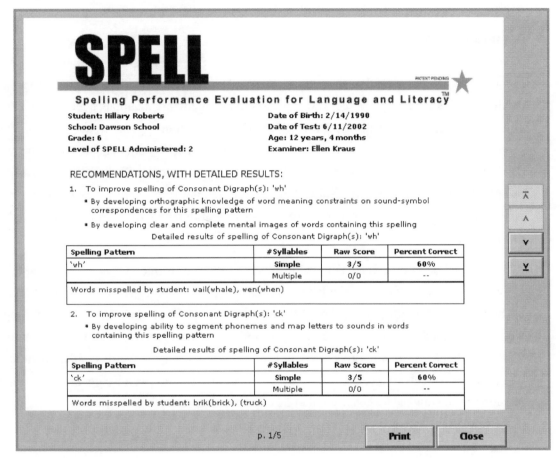

Student Information

The student's identifying information, as entered by the examiner in the Student Information Form, and the level of *SPELL* administered to the individual student is displayed at the top of the *SPELL* Recommendations Report.

Recommendations

The spelling patterns for which the student failed to meet the 60% criterion are listed in order of developmental sequence; this is the recommended order for spelling instruction. The educator ideally would select three to four spelling patterns and would provide instruction or remediation to target and stabilize these spelling patterns before moving on to the next three to four spellings patterns.

For each spelling pattern listed on the *SPELL* Recommendations Report, *SPELL* provides a customized learning objective for the individual student, based on that student's most frequent type of error when spelling the target pattern. The learning objective for each spelling pattern is derived from *SPELL*'s analysis of which available language knowledge domains the speller is and is not using to spell that spelling pattern. Thus, educators can optimally tailor instruction or remediation to the individual student and for a specific spelling pattern.

Detailed Results

Recommendations are triggered when the student fails to meet a criterion calculated across all possible spellings of a particular spelling pattern. The Recommendations Report provides a detailed breakdown of the raw scores within a spelling pattern. For example, a recommendation will be provided for the spelling pattern "Within-Word Doubling: *pp, bb, tt, dd*" if the student scores 60% or below across all spellings of *pp, bb, tt, dd*. The Recommendations Report will detail the raw scores for each of these four individual spellings in the "Within-Word Doubling: *pp, bb, tt, dd*" spelling pattern. **Note:** A particular spelling (e.g., *"pp"*) may be listed even when this particular spelling pattern was not assessed at the level of *SPELL* administered to the student.

In Level 1 and Level 2, the detailed results are further broken down according to number of syllables in the target word: single vs. multiple. In Level 3 and Level 4, the detailed results are broken down according to word type: simple vs. complex. For the *SPELL* assessment, simple words are defined as single-morpheme words without an unstressed, schwa vowel. Complex words are defined as multimorphemic words and single-morpheme words containing at least one unstressed, schwa vowel. In all cases, the examiner should exercise conservative inter-pretation of the raw data when a small number of opportunities for measurement are indicated in the raw data.

The breakdown of data according to word type can be useful when *SPELL* makes the rec-ommendation "This student not ready for learning how to spell inflected or derived words." Since spelling of inflected and derived words requires adequate ability to spell base words, *SPELL* will recommend that a student is not ready for spelling inflected or derived words when the assessment results indicate that the student has not achieved adequate proficiency with spelling of base words. When *SPELL* recommends that the student is not ready for learning how to spell inflected or derived words, the examiner will want to focus spelling instruction on spelling patterns in base words. The examiner should then disregard the errors in complex words and analyze the errors in simple words only, as the results and recommendations for a particular spelling pattern may be skewed by errors introduced when spelling inflected or derived words. For those spelling patterns with a minimal number of occurrences in simple words, the examiner might consider supplementing the results reported in *SPELL* with addi-tional informal testing.

Words Misspelled by Student

The *SPELL* Recommendations Report also lists the words misspelled by the student, and the student's misspellings of these words, for each spelling pattern. This information can provide valuable additional information and can be used by the educator to further tailor instruction for the individual student. For example, examination of the individual word misspellings may reveal that the student has difficulty with a particular spelling pattern in a specific phonetic context. If so, the educator should create word lists for spelling instruction that focus on that particular phonetic context. As with any test, the educator should take care to avoid or minimize use of the *SPELL* test items in the student's instructional program, as this could invalidate results of future administrations of *SPELL*.

Note: It is possible that more than one error for a particular spelling pattern can occur within the same word. When this occurs, number of errors and number of words listed will not be the same.

Note: While *SPELL* prescribes a learning objective based on the most frequently occurring type of error, all words in which the target pattern was misspelled, regardless of type of error, are listed.

Note: Pending the results of the **Spell Book II Module,** *SPELL* will recommend either to teach the student about semantic relationships between base words and inflected and derived forms or to encourage the student to use his or her knowledge of base-word spelling to correctly spell inflected and derived forms. In either case, it is incumbent upon the specialist to first establish that the student is proficient in spelling a particular base word before teaching the student about a semantic relationship and before teaching the student to use his or her knowledge of the semantic relationship to correctly spell the inflected or derived forms. Again, the specialist should take care to avoid or minimize use of the *SPELL* test items in the student's instructional program, as this could invalidate results of future administrations of *SPELL*.

Sharing the Results

With Students

Instruction and remediation of spelling skills involves active attention to the knowledge and strategies needed to become a successful speller. Although the specialist or classroom teacher provides the necessary information and practice activities to acquire new spelling skills, students must be active and willing learners to ensure that this new knowledge is acquired and used in everyday situations. Typically, when students understand the purpose and rationale for any instructional program, success with the program is increased. It is recommended, therefore, that the results of *SPELL* be shared with students.

When sharing the results of *SPELL* with a student, it is important to provide information about the student's strengths as well as the student's areas of need or challenge. Using the Results Report provided by *SPELL*, the specialist can begin by sharing with the student the areas of spelling development that he or she has already successfully developed. The specialist can then use these areas of student success as a springboard for discussing areas of spelling development that must still be acquired by the student. It is recommended that the specialist provide abundant examples to clarify the purpose of the intended instructional program. Clearly explaining how knowledge and strategies can increase the student's spelling abilities in specific ways allows the student to become an active partner in the process of establishing customized objectives and working toward meeting those objectives.

When discussing the *SPELL* results, the specialist needs to determine the appropriate terms to use. For older students (i.e., those in Grades 5–12 and adults), use of key terms, such as *phonological awareness* and *morphological knowledge,* is encouraged since they allow the specialist to be more direct and place the student in the role of a knowledgeable partner in the instructional or remedial process. For younger students (i.e., those in Grade 4 and younger), the specialist needs to determine whether the use of novel or unfamiliar terms may confuse the student or draw focus away from the learning objectives.

With Classroom Teachers

The importance of spelling in the classroom cannot be overemphasized. Students are often judged on their spelling, both on spelling tests and on other written work. Weak spelling skills can interfere with a student's ability to effectively communicate thoughts and feelings to others in writing. When a student struggles with how to spell words correctly, other aspects of his or her writing, such as grammar, organization, and clarity, are also negatively affected. It is critical, then, that classroom teachers understand students' present spelling capabilities, the areas that require improvement, and the factors that may be positively or negatively affecting their spelling. Thus, the specialist should share students' *SPELL* results with classroom teachers.

The specialist should monitor classroom teachers' familiarity with the assessment procedures associated with *SPELL*. Explanation and use of key terms, such as *phonological awareness* and *morphological knowledge,* is encouraged. Use of these terms allows the specialist to be more direct and facilitates the classroom teacher's role as a knowledgeable partner in the instructional or remedial process. The specialist can highlight beneficial activities already used by the classroom teacher or can suggest new and appropriate activities that can be integrated into the existing classroom curriculum.

Under *Management Tools, SPELL* provides a handy letter-style report that can be used to share results with classroom teachers. This letter, along with an individual student's *SPELL* report, should be reviewed with classroom teachers during discussions of students' spelling evaluations. The examiner may also wish to share a copy of *Suggestions for Implementing Spelling Recommendations into the Language Arts Curriculum* (Appendix B) and *Examples and Definitions of Spelling Terms for Parents and Teachers* (Appendix C) with the teacher. These documents are available in printed form in the Appendices in this manual and in electronic form on the *SPELL* CD-ROM.

Sample Letter to Teachers

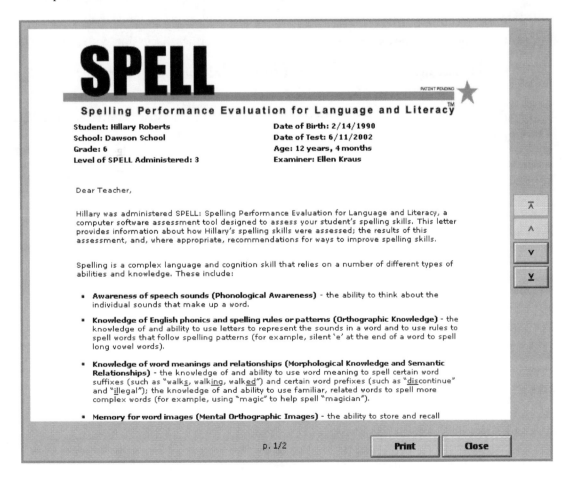

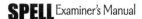

With Parents

Many parents express concern about their child's spelling capabilities. They likely are interested in learning more about their child's spelling abilities and what they can do to improve them. Educational objectives often are more successfully accomplished when everyone involved with the student—the specialist, the classroom teacher, and the parent—is a knowledgeable and active participant in the student's instructional program. Thus, the specialist should share the results of *SPELL* with students' parents.

It is important that numerous examples and definitions of terms (refer to the Glossary as necessary) be presented throughout the discussion of the results. Again, the specialist should emphasize both the strengths and the challenges or areas of need that a student demonstrates in spelling. The specialist and the classroom teacher may decide that it is appropriate to provide parents with tasks or activities that can be done in the home. However, even when home-based activities are not deemed appropriate, it remains crucial that parents be aware and supportive of the educational objectives set forth by *SPELL* and implemented by the specialist and the classroom teacher.

Under *Management Tools, SPELL* provides a convenient letter-style report that can be used to share results with parents. This letter, written in easy-to-understand language, provides a written record of the assessment and a springboard for further discussion with parents.

The examiner may also wish to share a copy of *Examples and Definitions of Spelling Terms for Parents and Teachers* (Appendix C) with the parents. This document is available in printed form in the Appendices section of this manual and in electronic form on the *SPELL* CD-ROM.

Sample Letter to Parents

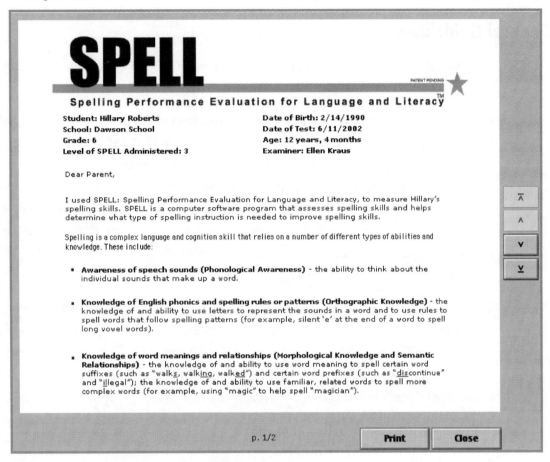

Instruction and Remediation

General Guidelines

Educators can use these basic instruction and remediation principles to guide them in their work of facilitating spelling development.

- **Instruction and remediation practices should be guided by a well-developed knowledge of spelling development and the factors that influence spelling**—Spelling acquisition studies suggest that spelling development is a self-generated process of relating and representing spoken language into its written form. This process occurs largely due to active attention to the phonological, orthographic, morphological, and semantic elements of spoken and written language. Knowledge of how these elements of language contribute to the development of spelling is crucial when planning activities to teach or improve spelling skills.

- **Spelling instruction and remediation should be guided by a specialist's theory of learning**—Although different learning theories exist, a social-constructivist theory appears to best explain language learning. This theory proposes that optimal learning occurs when viewed as a jointly constructed process between two or more individuals. In the case of spelling instruction and remediation, specialists guide students' learning by providing activities and situations that encourage them to use their current abilities to gain additional spelling strategies and knowledge. The authors of *SPELL* advocate the social-constructivist viewpoint for literacy learning in general, and for spelling instruction and remediation in particular, because of evidence from effective literacy intervention practices that supports this theory. Without any theory guiding instruction and remediation practices, specialists are likely to provide learning opportunities that do not meet the learning needs of the individuals served.

- **Spelling instruction and remediation should encourage self-discovery of spelling rules and patterns while simultaneously directing focused attention to the properties of both spoken and written language**—Educators should actively model the spelling skills to be learned and provide varying support for students' learning attempts based on their current level of ability. Because of the intimate relationship between spelling and reading, integration of these two literacy skills in instruction and remediation should be achieved.

- **Incorrect views of spelling should be changed**—Unfortunately, some consider spelling a skill that is learned "mysteriously" and that cannot be taught. Others believe that the English spelling system is completely illogical or too complex for study. Still others may assume that students who are poor at spelling cannot make progress in developing better spelling abilities. The specialist must be prepared to argue against these incorrect views of spelling in order to help students and other educators working with students improve students' spelling abilities. Helping others change their views on spelling is particularly important because of the negative effects these views can have on students' self-esteem and self-image as writers.

- **Students' perceptions of their spelling abilities should be acknowledged**— Because students who struggle with spelling often are highly aware of their abilities compared to those of their peers, they are likely to develop a poor self-image of themselves as spellers. The specialist should continually provide descriptive and positive feedback to students to encourage their awareness of the skills being learned and the progress achieved. By listening to the frustrations experienced in the past, encouraging them to take an active role in improving their skills, and acknowledging their attempts and struggles, the specialist may facilitate a change in students' self-images as spellers, thus increasing the chances that motivation and effort will increase.

- **The use of metacognitive and self-regulation strategies should be encouraged**— Metacognitive and self-regulation strategies include the ability to manage one's performance on a task, such as using positive self-talk while engaged in a task, efficiently organizing time, and effectively planning and monitoring the task at hand. These strategies are important to incorporate in spelling instruction and remediation. For example, students should be required to think about their new spelling strategies each time they must spell an unfamiliar word. The specialist should encourage students to consider all possible strategies learned and to choose the best strategy or strategies to use when attempting to spell the unfamiliar word. Additionally, students should be encouraged to proof unfamiliar spellings, using their newly learned spelling strategies to confirm the appropriateness of the attempted spelling.

- **Self-monitoring, focus, and effort on a task should be encouraged to stabilize use of spelling knowledge**—Students with poor spelling skills are poor monitors and proofreaders of their own spelling. Once a student has established and developed the language knowledge domains required for correct spelling, they will likely continue to exhibit occasional misspellings in their written work. These students benefit greatly from activities that encourage heightened effort and focus on tasks and self-monitoring and correction of their written work.

The information in Part I of the *SPELL Examiner's Manual,* as well as the resources listed in the "Helpful Resources" section should guide educators in helping others change their views of spelling. Additionally, some of these resources (e.g., Apel & Masterson, 1997; Apel & Swank, 1999; Webster, 1981) provide guidelines for encouraging and supporting students' positive self-images of themselves as spellers and helping them develop useful metacognitive and self-regulation strategies.

35

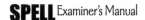

Customized Learning Objectives and Related Spelling Activities

SPELL provides specific, customized learning objectives for each student who completes the program. The learning objectives encourage spelling activities that are most appropriate for the individual student based on the identified factors that underlie that student's misspellings. Possible causes for misspellings include deficiencies in:

★ **Phonological Awareness and Alphabetic Principle**

- Ability to segment words into syllables and phonemes and map letters to sounds

- Ability to recognize meaningful contrasts between sounds and map letters to sounds

★ **Orthographic Knowledge**

- Knowledge of phoneme-grapheme (sound-symbol) correspondences

- Knowledge of letter patterns and spelling rules

- Knowledge of phonetic, positional, and semantic constraints on letter patterns

★ **Morphological Knowledge and Semantic Relationships**

- Knowledge of morphemes and morpheme-grapheme correspondences

- Knowledge of semantic relationships between base words and inflected forms

- Knowledge of semantic relationships between base words and derived forms

- Knowledge of rules for the modification of base words when spelling inflected forms

- Knowledge of rules for the modification of base words when spelling derived forms

★ **Mental Orthographic Memory**

- Long-term storage of clear and complete mental orthographic images (MOIs) of words

- Visual orientation of graphemes

The following sections discuss instruction and remediation principles for spelling activities within each of these language knowledge domains.

Phonological Awareness and Alphabetic Principle

One successful strategy for spelling involves breaking down words into syllables or phonemes and then spelling these smaller units with the appropriate grapheme or graphemes. Results of *SPELL* may indicate that a student requires spelling practice that involves word and syllable segmentation and mapping of letters to sounds. Thus, specific phonological awareness and alphabetic principle learning objectives may be recommended by *SPELL* to improve the student's spelling of a specific spelling pattern.

The following are phonological awareness and alphabetic principle learning objectives prescribed by SPELL.

To improve spelling of (<u>specific spelling pattern</u>):

- By developing ability to segment phonemes and map letters to sounds in words containing this spelling pattern

- By developing ability to segment syllables and map letters to sounds in words containing this spelling pattern

---

Some students may misspell words because they do not discriminate between phonemes in a meaningful way. For example, a student may not perceive a difference between short *e* and short *i* or the student may hear a phonetic (i.e., sound) difference between these two sounds but may not recognize the phonemic (i.e., meaning) difference between these two sounds. When this occurs, a student may spell two vowel phonemes with one grapheme. Results of *SPELL* testing may indicate that a student requires spelling practice that fosters recognition of meaningful contrasts and mapping of letters to sounds to improve spelling. Thus, specific learning objectives may be recommended to improve the student's spelling of a specific spelling pattern.

The following are phonological awareness and alphabetic principle learning objectives prescribed by SPELL.

To improve spelling of (<u>specific spelling pattern</u>):

- By developing ability to recognize meaningful vowel contrasts and map letters to sounds in words containing this spelling pattern

- By developing ability to recognize meaningful contrasts between vocalic liquids and vowels and map letters to sounds in words containing this spelling pattern

---

When *SPELL*'s learning objectives for spelling instruction include segmenting phonemes and syllables and mapping letters to sounds and recognizing meaningful contrasts and mapping letters to sounds, the examiner will want to follow these general guidelines for spelling instruction:

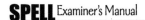

- **Link segmentation and discrimination activities to spelling**—Specialists should implement spelling activities that target the specific segmentation and discrimination difficulties manifested in the individual's spelling errors. For example, *SPELL* may prescribe a learning objective to improve spelling of liquid and nasal clusters (as found in a word like *black)* by developing the student's ability to segment these specific phonemes and map letters to sounds in words containing this spelling pattern. In this case, the specialist should develop segmentation spelling tasks that highlight and inform the individual about the presence of nasal and liquid clusters in words and how those clusters are represented in the written word.

- **Consider phoneme properties**—The properties of the target phoneme or phonological structure may influence spelling intervention activities. Targets that contain sonorants (vowel-like consonants, such as nasals and liquids) and clusters are more difficult to segment and spell than targets representing other features, such as stops (e.g., /p/ and /b/) and sibilants (e.g., /s/ and /ʃ/). Short vowels are more difficult to discriminate and spell than long vowels. *SPELL* may prescribe several learning objectives to improve spelling by developing the student's ability to segment or recognize specific phonemes and map letters to sounds. The specialist will want to sequence the order of spelling patterns that are presented in spelling instruction so as to proceed from less challenging to more challenging spelling patterns based upon phoneme properties.

- **Target meaningful differences signaled by spelling**—Spelling instruction or remediation activities that foster phoneme discrimination necessarily require active attention to the meaning differences signaled by each phoneme/grapheme in question. For example, *SPELL* may prescribe a learning objective to improve spelling of short vowel *e* by developing the student's ability to recognize a meaningful vowel contrast and map letters to sounds in words containing this spelling pattern. The specialist can use minimal pairs to facilitate a student's understanding of the meaningful differences signaled by two different phonemes. For example, if a student consistently uses the grapheme *i* for words containing the short *e* vowel (e.g., *bet* misspelled as *bit)*, then activities should require the student to accurately identify each word in minimal word pairs within the meaningful context in which each word is used.

Orthographic Knowledge

Orthographic knowledge involves the spelling rules or strategies required to convert spoken language to written language. This knowledge involves recognizing the appropriate graphemes used to represent different phonemes (sound-symbol correspondences), understanding which graphemes or grapheme combinations can occur in different phonetic contexts (e.g., the /dʒ/ sound in *fudge* must be spelled with *dge* because it follows a short vowel, unlike the /ʤ/ in *huge,* which follows a long vowel) and understanding which grapheme or grapheme combinations can occur in different positions of a word (e.g., the /k/ sound can never be spelled with *ck* at the beginning of a word). After careful analyses, *SPELL* may recommend specific learning objectives to facilitate a student's orthographic knowledge to improve spelling skills for a specific spelling pattern.

The following are orthographic knowledge learning objectives prescribed by SPELL.

To improve spelling of (specific spelling pattern):

- By developing orthographic knowledge of sound-symbol correspondences for this spelling pattern

- By developing orthographic knowledge of word meaning constraints on sound-symbol correspondences

- By developing orthographic knowledge of word meaning constraints to correct over-generalized use of morpheme -ed to spell word final /t, d/

- By developing orthographic knowledge about when to use silent e at end of word when spelling long vowel words

- By developing orthographic knowledge of long vs. short vowel principles for this spelling pattern

- By developing orthographic knowledge of syllable and word position constraints on sound-symbol correspondences

- By developing orthographic knowledge of rules for conditioning silent e

- By developing orthographic knowledge of sound-symbol correspondences for this spelling pattern, with specific attention to correct pronunciation of /r, l/ in clusters so as to discourage insertion of vowels when spelling this liquid cluster spelling pattern

- By developing orthographic knowledge of sound-symbol correspondences, specifically not to use consonant letters to represent sounds that are not perceived to be present

- By improving orthographic knowledge, specifically not to use vowel and consonant letters to represent sounds that are not perceived to be present

---

These objectives, although focusing on specific rules or patterns of orthography, have as their core feature the need to develop an understanding of English spelling conventions (Appendix D includes all of the orthographic spelling patterns evaluated by the *SPELL* program.) The following set of principles should be used to facilitate students' knowledge of English orthography during spelling activities.

- **Encourage self-discovery of orthographic rules**—Developing knowledge for orthographic rules typically involves self-discovery approaches, often through the use of word-sorting activities. In these activities, students are encouraged to search for, or

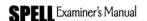

sort by, specific phoneme-grapheme patterns or spelling rules. Students then use this knowledge to guide the spelling of other words that follow the same patterns and rules.

- **Target contrasting rules**—Students should be presented with two sets of words representing two specific orthographic patterns or rules (e.g., short *i* and long *i* vowel words, like *pit/kite)*. Through modeling and guidance from the educator, the student is encouraged to read the words aloud, discuss similarities or differences between the words, and place the words into separate columns according to the shared or common feature.

- **Describe rules**—Once a student has accurately grouped words by their shared or common feature, the student should be encouraged to describe the rule (e.g., *i* by itself is a short vowel sound, but *i* + a consonant + *e* results in a long vowel sound).

- **Establish keywords**—After discovering the rule that depicts the sets of words, the student should be encouraged to pick keywords. The keywords are words that the student knows how to spell and can be recalled easily to act as models or reminders for the rule.

- **Practice new rules in controlled writing tasks**—The educator should dictate simple sentences containing targeted spelling rules and encourage the student to use the newly learned rules and keywords to guide spelling of target words.

- **Implement word searches**—The student can be encouraged to search for words in favorite or required texts and identify those words that are spelled according to the newly learned rule. The keywords can be used to confirm correct use of the rules.

- **Attend to specific word-position rules**—Certain orthographic rules specify positional constraints on the use of graphemes to represent phonemes. For example, the digraph *ck* may only occur in the middle and end of English words; it never occurs in the beginning. The sorting activities discussed above also can be used to differentiate specific word-position and grapheme-combining rules. By presenting words that differ based on the use of specific graphemes or digraphs in specific word positions, students can acquire these rules as well.

- **Choose target rules according to spelling development**—As in other areas of language, specialists should use their knowledge of spelling development to guide the facilitation of orthographic knowledge.

Morphological Knowledge and Semantic Relationships

Morphological knowledge includes the knowledge of morphemes and morpheme-grapheme correspondences, knowledge of semantic relationships between base words and their inflected or derived forms, and knowledge of rules for modifying a base word when spelling an inflected or derived form. Knowledge of how to spell a base word, coupled with the knowledge of how inflectional and derivational markers are spelled and how they modify base words, guides the spelling of inflected and derived forms. The *SPELL* analysis may suggest that a student improve the ability to use morphological knowledge to spell complex words. Thus specific morphological knowledge learning objectives may be recommended by *SPELL* to increase the student's skills with a specific spelling pattern.

The following are morphological knowledge learning objectives prescribed by SPELL.

To improve spelling of (<u>specific spelling pattern</u>):

- By developing morphological knowledge of rules for spelling these inflectional morphemes; supplement morphological knowledge with phonological awareness, orthographic knowledge, and mental orthographic images when appropriate

- By developing morphological knowledge of rules for modifying base words when adding these inflectional morphemes

- By developing morphological knowledge of semantic relationships between base words and inflected forms and using knowledge of base word spelling to spell words with these inflectional morphemes

- By using knowledge of base word spelling when spelling words with these inflectional morphemes

- By developing and using all knowledge sources (phonological, orthographic, and morphological) and by developing mental orthographic images for irregular past tense verbs

- By developing morphological knowledge of rules for spelling derivational morphemes; supplement morphological knowledge with phonological awareness, orthographic knowledge and mental orthographic images when appropriate

- By developing morphological knowledge of rules for modifying base words when spelling derived forms with this transparency

- By developing morphological knowledge of semantic relationships between base words and derived forms and using knowledge of base word spelling to spell derived forms with this transparency

- By using knowledge of base word spelling when spelling derived forms with this transparency

---

These objectives cover both inflectional and derivational morphological knowledge. It is possible that *SPELL* will recommend only one type of morphological knowledge. If both types of morphological knowledge are recommended, the educator should consider first developing knowledge of inflectional morphology and then progress to developing knowledge of derivational morphology. (Appendix E includes all of the morphologic spelling patterns evaluated by the *SPELL* program.) The following set of principles should be used to facilitate students' knowledge of semantic relationships and morphology during spelling activities.

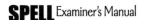

- **Link meaning between words**—As students spell more complex words, knowledge for the morphological and semantic relationships among words may facilitate correct spelling. For example, the inflected and derived words *product, producer,* and *production* are all related to one another in meaning and have as their core the base word *produce.* Although *product* and *production* sound different than *produce,* and all three inflected and derived words are spelled differently, knowledge for the spelling of the base word that they share should facilitate their correct spelling. Thus, the educator should heighten students' awareness of the morphological and semantic relationships among words.

- **Identify relationships**—When first addressing morphological knowledge, the educator should provide students with a simple base word (e.g., *act)* and ask them to think of all words that seem to be related to the base word (e.g., *act, acting, actor, action).* The students should be encouraged to discuss what common meaning the words share. After this general introduction, the educator should focus the students' attention on inflectional or derivational morphology, depending on the objectives suggested by *SPELL.*

- **Heighten awareness for inflectional morphology**—After the general introduction, the educator should draw attention to the specific inflectional marker recommended by *SPELL* for improvement (e.g., *-ed, -ing, -s)* and ask students to discuss its meaning. To facilitate this discussion, multiple base words should be paired with this target inflectional marker and the students should be encouraged to discuss how the meaning of each base word is changed similarly with its addition. For example, when *-ed* is added to the base words *jump, hug,* and *pat,* the meaning of each word implies an action that has already occurred.

- **Target correct spelling of inflections**—If the *SPELL* recommendations suggest that a student needs to learn the correct spelling for a specific inflectional marker, the educator should provide practice for spelling the target inflection. Additionally, the educator should draw attention to the different phonemes that may be heard when adding the inflectional marker to a base word. In the above examples, the *-ed* represents /t/, /d/, and /ɪd/.

- **Target inflectional spelling patterns**—When students are unaware of the specific orthographic rules for combining base words and inflections, a sorting task should be used. With this task, students can be provided with sets of words that represent contrasting rules for adding an inflectional marker. For example, students may be given words that are modified when adding an *-ed* (e.g., *hope/hoped, stop/stopped)* and those that are not (e.g., *jump/jumped, scold/scolded).*

- **Contrast inflected with noninflected word endings**—When students overgeneralize the use of inflectional markers (e.g., *-ed)* to words whose endings sound similar to inflected words (e.g., spelling *trust* as *trussed)*, the educator should review the purpose of the inflected marker (in this case, to note past tense) with the student. A sorting task of pictured items that contain inflected (e.g., *fanned)* and noninflected but similarly sounding words (e.g., *brand)* can be used to highlight words that signal a particular time or aspect and those that do not. Subsequently, the spelling rules that apply to the inflected words can be reviewed and a discussion can be held regarding how to spell the words that do not contain an inflectional marker.

- **Heighten awareness of derivational morphology**—After the general introduction, the educator should highlight the fact that some derived words are similar to the base word in sound and spelling (e.g., *royalty/royal)*, some are similar in spelling but differ in sound (e.g., *magician/magic)*, some are similar in sound but differ in spelling (e.g., *continue/continuous)*, and others differ in both sound and spelling (e.g., *description/describe)*. Regardless of any changes to sound or spelling, however, the shared or common meaning among the words remains the same.

- **Identify commonalities among base words and derived forms**—When a student identifies the meaning relationship between a base word and its derived form, the educator should guide the student in identifying the common spelling shared by each word. For example, the educator can prompt the student to identify how *loyal* is contained in *loyalty*. Thus, knowledge of how to spell *loyal* guides the spelling of *loyalty*. Subsequently, other familiar base words can be presented and the student can be encouraged to spell a derived form using the base word as a guide.

- **Control for transparency of derivational forms**—When facilitating a student's use of base words to spell derived forms, derived forms that involve no change to the sound or spelling of the base word should be presented first (e.g., *friend, friendly)*. These word pairs are considered to be transparent because of the lack of orthographic or phonemic differences between the base word and its derived forms. Once the student understands how to use the base word to make decisions about the spelling of a transparent derived form, subsequent examples can be used that are less transparent. These examples could include spelling derived forms that involve changes only to the spelling of the base word (e.g., *penny, penniless)*, then changes only in the pronunciation of the base word (e.g., *magic, magician)*, and finally, changes to both the spelling and pronunciation of the base word (e.g., *admit, admission)*.

Mental Orthographic Memory

Mental orthographic images (MOIs) are the mental images of word spellings that individuals store in memory after repeated exposures. Although many images are of words that can be spelled using knowledge of phonology, orthography, semantic relationships, or morphology,

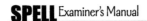

some images represent words for which the use of these language knowledge domains will result in either partial or complete misspelling of the word. That is, certain words must be learned through repeated exposures to the word with careful attention to the spelling such that an adequate and complete image of the word can be recalled later. Thus, *SPELL* may recommend specific learning objectives for improving a student's mental orthographic memory of a specific spelling pattern when other spelling strategies would not be useful or productive.

The following are mental orthographic memory learning objectives prescribed by SPELL.

To improve spelling of (<u>specific spelling pattern</u>):

- By developing clear and complete mental images of words containing this spelling pattern

- By developing clear and complete mental images of words containing this spelling pattern, with specific attention to reversal of b/d

---

The following set of principles should be used when *SPELL* recommends instruction to facilitate mental orthographic images.

- **Discuss the characteristics of the word**—The educator should encourage the student to look at a target word and discuss its characteristics. For example, the discussion might focus on the number of vowels and consonants in the words and the configuration of the word (one "tall" grapheme followed by two "short" graphemes, followed by one tall grapheme, such as in *deal*).

- **Spell the word with the printed form present**—While viewing the word, the educator should first model and then require the student to spell the word both forward and backward. The latter strategy is used to encourage the student's attention to each individual grapheme, rather than viewing the word as a whole unit.

- **Visualize the word**—After the student has discussed the characteristics of the word and practiced spelling it forward and backward while the printed word is visible, the printed form should be removed and the student should be asked to visualize the word. The educator should guide the student through another discussion of the characteristics of the word while the student pictures the word.

- **Spell the word without the printed form present**—After a discussion of the characteristics, the student should spell the word forward and then backward. Successful forward and backward spelling of the word suggests that the student has adequately stored a clear image of each individual grapheme in the correct sequence. Subsequent practice with this strategy over time, with repeated requests to picture words practiced previously, should ensure more complete and clear representations of spellings in the student's memory.

Other Considerations for Spelling Instruction

Students who score above 60% and below 100% correct for a particular spelling pattern on *SPELL* do not require explicit and direct instruction in a particular knowledge source at the single-word level. Instead, these students who exhibit occasional misspellings would benefit more from intervention activities that promote their consistent application of knowledge sources in their written work. These students will benefit greatly from activities that encourage heightened effort and focus on task and self-monitoring and correction of their written work to stabilize use of their spelling knowledge.

Part II
User Guide

Getting Started with *SPELL*

System Requirements

Before installing *SPELL*, check to be sure that your system meets these minimum system requirements.

Windows 98/ME

Pentium II, 233 MHz or higher

32 MB RAM (64 MB recommended)

10 MB free hard disk space (200 MB free for virtual memory)

16-bit color monitor

Windows-compatible sound card

4x CD-ROM drive

Windows 2000/XP

Pentium II, 233 MHz or higher

64 MB RAM (128 MB recommended)

10 MB free hard disk space

16-bit color monitor

Windows-compatible sound card

4x CD-ROM drive

Macintosh

MacOS 8.6 or higher*

Power PC 250 MHz processor or higher (G3 recommended)

24 MB available memory (32 MB recommended)

10 MB free hard disk space

16-bit color monitor

4x CD-ROM drive

---

*While the application may run on Mac OSX, this platform is not yet supported for Macromedia applications. (See *http://www.macromedia.com/support/director/ts /documents/director_osx.htm for details*.)

Installation

Windows

1. Insert the CD-ROM into your computer's CD-ROM drive.

2. Double-click the **My Computer** icon.

3. Double-click the **SPELL** CD icon (unless the directory window for the CD is already displayed).

4. Double-click the **Setup** icon.

5. Follow the onscreen setup instructions.

Macintosh

1. Insert the CD-ROM into your computer's CD-ROM drive.

2. Double-click the **SPELL** CD icon (unless the directory window for the CD is already displayed).

Set Up

Storing Data

The student data records are stored in two files on your hard drive. It is recommended that you regularly copy the files to a floppy disk or other external storage medium for added protection against loss.

In Windows, the files are stored in:
HD:\Program Files\Learning By Design\SPELL\daata\SPL_TRX.v12
HD:\Program Files\Learning By Design\SPELL\daata\STUDENTS.v12

On Macintosh, the files are stored in:
Learning By Design:SPELL:daata:SPL_TRX.v12
LearningByDesign:SPELL:daata:STUDENTS.v12

Setting Monitor Resolution

The recommended monitor resolution for *SPELL* is 800 × 600. In Windows, from the **Start** menu, select **Control Panel, Display: Settings** and select 800 × 600 display resolution. Click **Apply.** On a Macintosh, from the apple menu, select **Control Panel** and choose **Monitor** to select 800 × 600 display resolution.

Launching the *SPELL* Program

Once *SPELL* has been installed, you are ready to launch the program. **Note:** The *SPELL* CD-ROM must be in the CD drive to run the program.

Windows

1. Insert the CD-ROM into your computer's CD drive.

2. From the Start menu, select Programs, Learning By Design, SPELL, and click on SPELL.

Macintosh

1. Insert the CD-ROM into your computer's CD drive.

2. Navigate to and select the **Learning By Design** folder on your hard drive.

3. Double-click on the **SPELL** folder.

4. Double-click on the **Start** program icon.

Entering a Password

The first time you launch the *SPELL* program you will be asked to enter a personal password between 5 and 10 characters in length. You will be asked to retype your chosen password into the verification screen. This password will be required to create a new student record, to begin and resume testing for a student, and to access and manage student records using the *Management Tools*. The password security ensures confidentiality of student records and validity and reliability of the data. Once you decide on a password, you may wish to write it in the box below for future reference.

My Password

Changing Your Password

If you forget or wish to change your password, simply enter "VERDI" when prompted for a password. After you enter this code, you will be prompted to enter a new password. A verification screen will be displayed to verify your new password.

Main Menu

Each time you start *SPELL*, the ***Main Menu*** will be displayed. From the ***Main Menu,*** you can select one of four options: *Test New Student, Resume Testing, Management Tools,* or *Examiner Preview.*

Test New Student

Test New Student allows you to create a student data record and to begin testing a new student. Use this feature each time you test a new student with *SPELL*.

Main Menu

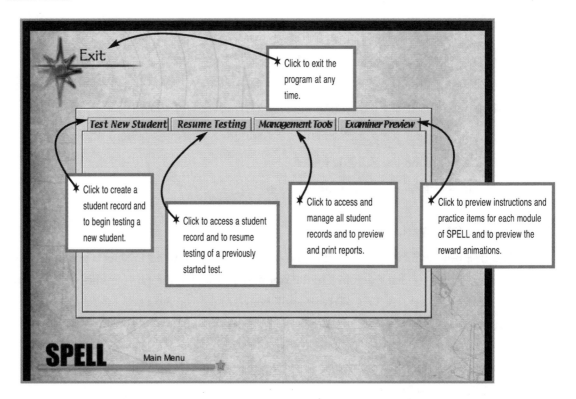

Student Information Form, #1

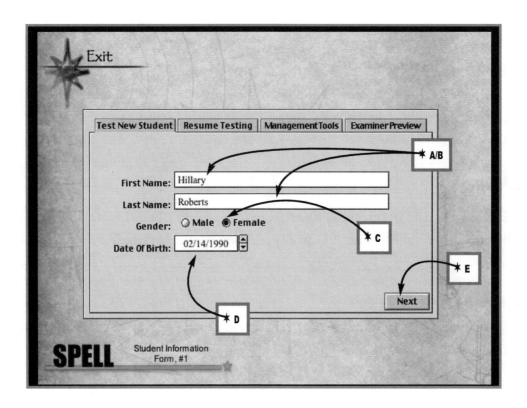

Launching Test New Student

Click the *Test New Student* folder tab on the **Main Menu** to create a student data record and to begin testing a new student. You will be prompted to enter your password.

Completing the Student Information Form

Before testing a new student, you will be asked to complete a Student Information Form. Completion of the Student Information Form will create a student data record for the new student. You will want to gather all the information listed below prior to completing the form. The Student Information Form consists of three parts.

On Student Information Form, #1, you will be required to enter the student's name, gender, and date of birth.

★ **A/B**   Type the student's first and last name into the appropriate data fields.

★ **C**   Indicate the student's gender by clicking on the appropriate radio button.

★ **D**   Enter the student's date of birth by first clicking on the date, month, or year. The selected date, month, or year will be highlighted in red. Use the up and down arrows to adjust the selected number.

★ **E**   Click **Next** to continue.

On Student Information Form, #2 (see page 54), you will be required to enter the name of the student's school or your clinic, the examiner's name, the student's grade, the student's spelling grade level (if known), and the date of testing.

★ **A/B**   Type in the appropriate data fields the school or clinic name and the examiner's name as you want them to appear on all *SPELL* reports.

★ **C**   Enter or select from list the student's grade (1–12 or Adult).

★ **D**   Enter or select from list the student's spelling grade level (Unknown or 4–12$^+$).

★ **E**   Enter the date of testing by first clicking on the date, month, or year. The selected date, month, or year will be highlighted in red. Use the up and down arrows to adjust the selected number.

★ **F**   Click **Next** to continue.

★ **G**   Click **Back** to return to a previous screen of the Student Information Form.

Student Information Form, #2

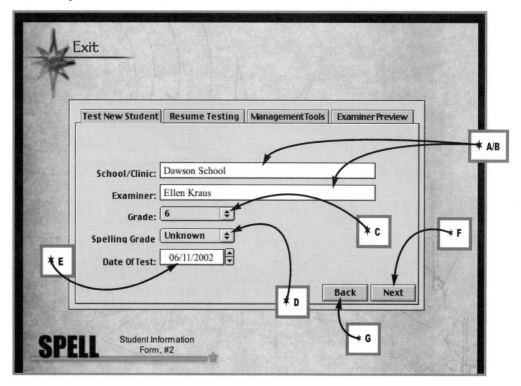

Student Information Form, #3

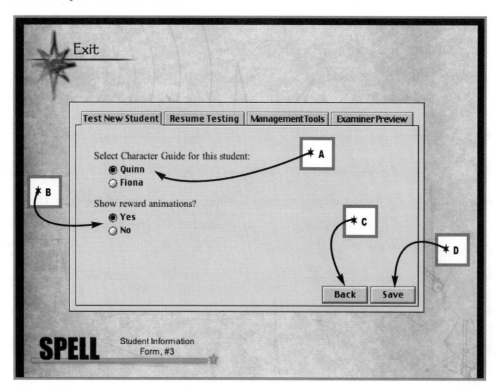

On Student Information Form, #3, you will be required to select a character guide and to choose whether reward animations will be provided for this new student.

★ **A**   Select a character guide by clicking on the appropriate radio button. The default setting is determined by the student's grade: Fiona is selected for Grades 3 and below; Quinn is selected for Grades 4–12 and adults.

★ **B**   Decide whether to show reward animations. You can make your selection by clicking on the appropriate radio button. The default setting is Yes.

★ **C**   Click **Back** to return to a previous Student Information Screen.

★ **D**   Click **Save** to store the student's information.

Note: You may cancel out of the Student Information Form at any time by clicking on another folder tab at the top of the Student Information Form. If you cancel out of the Student Information Form before saving the student data, no student data record will be created for the student and any information entered will be discarded.

Preparing the Student to Begin Testing

Once you have completed all three parts of the Student Information Form, the student information is displayed onscreen for easy verification that the proper student file has been stored. You will then be prompted to prepare the student to begin testing (see page 56). When this student is seated at the computer and ready to begin testing in the **Selector Module**, click **OK.** Click **Back** to return to the Student Information Form.

Resume Testing

Resume Testing allows you to access a student data record and to resume testing a student who previously began and did not complete the *SPELL* assessment (see page 56). This feature allows you to easily administer *SPELL* in more than one session. Use this feature each time a student returns to resume testing.

Note: Once a student completes the *SPELL* assessment, his or her name will be removed from the Student List under *Resume Testing*. Records for students who have completed the *SPELL* assessment can be accessed under *Management Tools*.

Launching Resume Testing

Click the *Resume Testing* folder tab on the ***Main Menu*** to access a student record and to resume testing. You will be prompted to enter your password.

Prepare to Begin Test

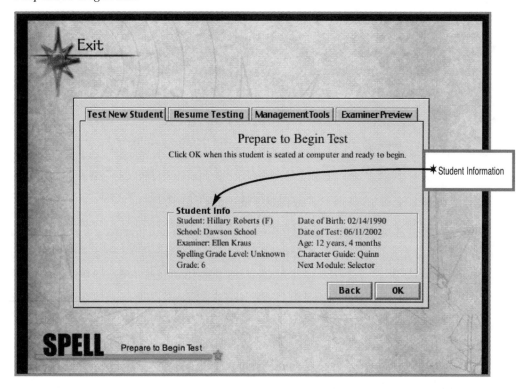

Resume Testing

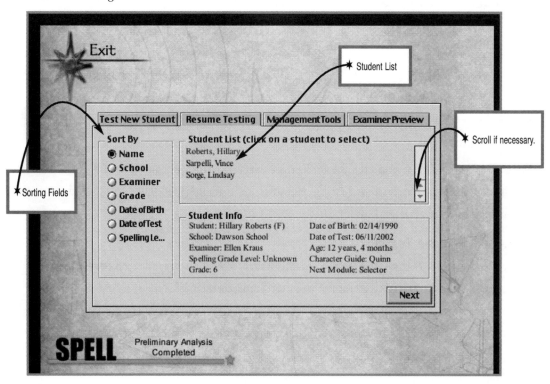

Selecting a Student to Resume Testing

After you enter your password, you will be asked to select from the Student List the name of the student who will resume testing. A list of all students who have begun and not yet completed *SPELL* appears onscreen. Use the scroll bar to view the complete list of names. To quickly locate a student name in the list, you may wish to sort the list by various fields: Name, School, Examiner, Grade, Date of Birth, Date of Test, or Spelling Grade Level. Click on the appropriate radio button to sort student records by data field. The default sort is by Name. To open the student's record, click on the desired name in the list and then click **Next.**

When a student record is open, the student's information is displayed onscreen for easy verification that the proper student data record file has been opened. Click **Next** to continue.

NOTE: You may cancel out of *Resume Testing* at any time by clicking on another folder tab.

Preparing the Student to Resume Testing

Once you have selected a student name and opened a student record, you will be prompted to prepare the student to resume testing. The student information is displayed onscreen for easy verification that the proper student data record file has been opened.

NOTE: If you wish to change or update any information in the student record, you may do so using *Management Tools*.

When this student is seated at the computer and ready to begin testing, click **OK.**

Prepare to Resume Test

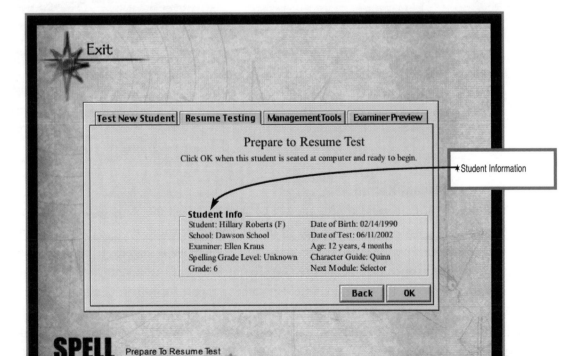

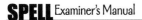

Management Tools

Management Tools allows you to access and manage student data records of students who have completed *SPELL* and to preview and print results and recommendations reports and letters for teachers and parents. You may also use this feature to access student records for students who have not completed *SPELL* when you wish to edit or delete the student data records.

Launching Management Tools

Click the *Management Tools* folder tab on the **Main Menu** to access student records and reports. You will be prompted to enter your password.

Management Tools: Editing/Deleting a Student Record

Exit

| Test New Student | Resume Testing | Management Tools | Examiner Preview |

Sort By
- ● Name
- ○ School
- ○ Examiner
- ○ Grade
- ○ Date of Birth
- ○ Date of Test
- ○ Spelling Le...

Student List (click on a student to select)
Roberts, Hillary
Sarpelli, Vince
Sorge, Lindsay

Student Info
Student: Hillary Roberts (F)   Date of Birth: 02/14/1990
School: Dawson School   Date of Test: 06/11/2002
Examiner: Ellen Kraus   Age: 12 years, 4 months
Spelling Grade Level: Unknown   Character Guide: Quinn
Grade: 6   Next Module: Selector

Select A Report... ◆ View/Print   Edit   Delete

★ Click to permanently delete a selected student's data record.

★ Click to Edit a student data record.

SPELL Management Tools

Selecting a Student Record

After selecting *Management Tools,* you will be asked to select the name of the student whose data record you wish to access. A list of all students for whom there exists a data record appears onscreen. Use the scroll bar to view the complete list of names. Click on the desired name in the list to open the student's record. To quickly locate a student name in the list, you may wish to sort the list by various fields: Name, School, Examiner, Grade, Date of Birth, Date of Test, or Spelling Grade Level. Click on the appropriate radio button to sort student records by data field. The default sort is by Student Name. When a student record is opened, the student's information is displayed onscreen for easy verification that the proper student data record file has been opened.

Management Tools: View/Print a Report

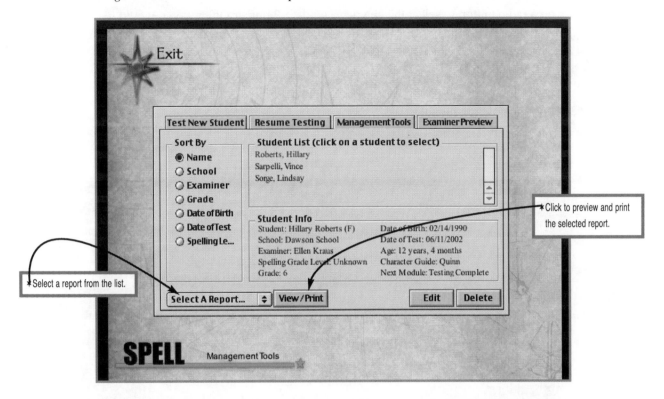

Note: You may cancel out of *Management Tools* at any time by clicking on another folder tab.

Selecting a Report or Letter

If the selected student has completed the *SPELL* test, you may use *Management Tools* to preview and print the following reports and letters: Results, Recommendations, Letter to Parents, or Letter to Teacher. (For a sample parent letter, see Appendix F; for a sample teacher letter, see Appendix G.) Select a report from the list in the lower left corner of the *Management Tools* screen.

Examiner Preview

The *Examiner Preview* feature allows you to preview instructions and practice items for each of the *SPELL* test modules and to preview the reward animations. Use this feature to familiarize yourself—and your students, if needed—with each of the *SPELL* test modules.

Launching Examiner Preview

Click the *Examiner Preview* folder tab on the **Main Menu** to preview instructions and practice items for each of the *SPELL* test modules and to preview the reward animations. No password is required.

Selecting a Character Guide for the Preview

Click on a radio button to select the character guide—Fiona or Quinn—you would like to see when you preview the selected modules.

Selecting a Module to Preview

Click on a button to preview a module or the motivational reward animations that are interspersed throughout the modules.

Examiner Preview

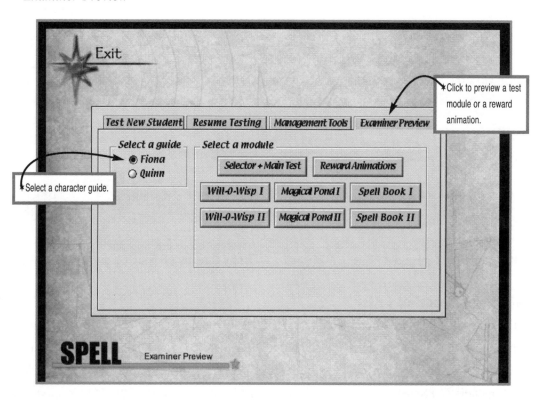

NOTE: You may cancel out of *Examiner Preview* at any time by clicking on another folder tab and you may cancel a module preview by clicking **Exit.**

Testing Modules

General Features

The following general features are available throughout the *SPELL* testing modules.

★ **A**   Click **Exit** to exit a testing module and return to the *Main Menu* at any time. The student's data will be saved when exiting a testing module.

★ **B/C**   Click **Pause** to suspend testing at any time. When clicked, the **Pause** button changes to **Resume.** This pausing option is not available during presentation of a practice or test item. The student may pause anytime before or after the verbal presentation. Click **Resume** to resume testing after pausing.

★ **D** Click **Repeat** to repeat the most recent instruction or the most recent practice or test item. A student may repeat a practice item an unlimited number of times. Test items may be repeated only once. **NOTE:** These features are disabled in the **Magical Pond I** and **Magical Pond II Modules.**

General Features of Testing Modules

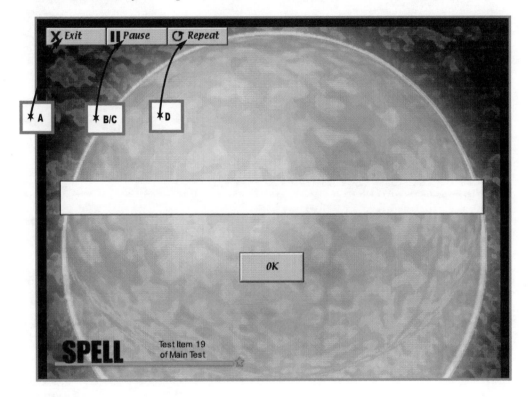

Status of Testing in Progress

When a student exits the *SPELL* assessment program before all testing is completed, a message window will appear with the student's current status of testing in progress (see page 62). Each of the assessment modules is listed onscreen, and the modules the student has already completed are checked. Any additional test modules that are not required for this student will be grayed out. *SPELL* makes decisions about which additional test modules are required during the **Preliminary Analysis Module** and also in real time as the student completes each additional test module. As such, the list of additional test modules to be completed is dynamic (i.e., additional test modules that were previously grayed out may later appear as modules to be administered to the student).

Status of Testing in Progress

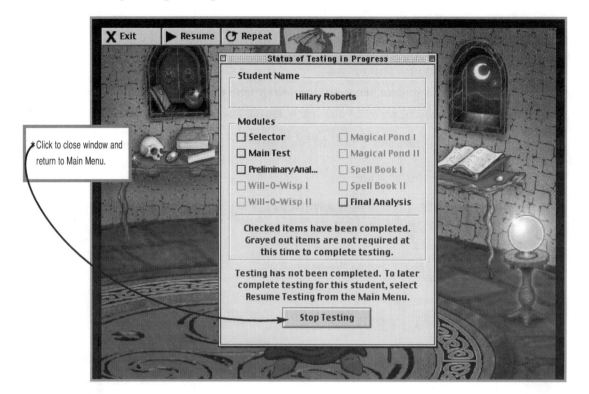

Student Assistance

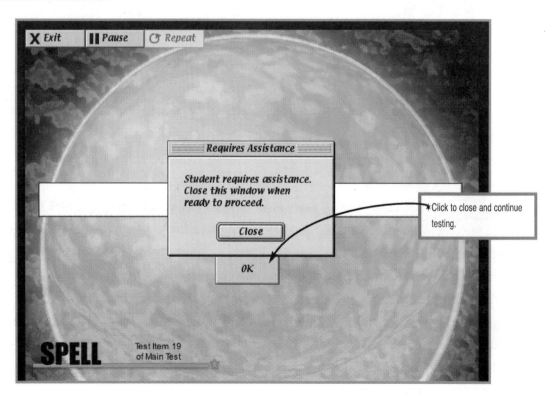

Student Requires Assistance

A message window will appear when the student does not make a response after two presentations of a practice or test item. At this time, you may provide general assistance (e.g., redirecting the student to the task and reviewing the instructions). Do not assist the student with how to respond to a specific test item. When the student is prepared to continue with the test, click **Close** and then click **OK.**

Administration

Sequence

The administration of *SPELL* follows the same sequence for all students: **Selector Module** → **Main Test Module** → **Preliminary Analysis Module** → **Additional Test Modules** (as needed) → **Final Analysis Module.** Students automatically flow into and through this sequence without the examiner adjusting any settings. Figure 2 illustrates the sequence in detail.

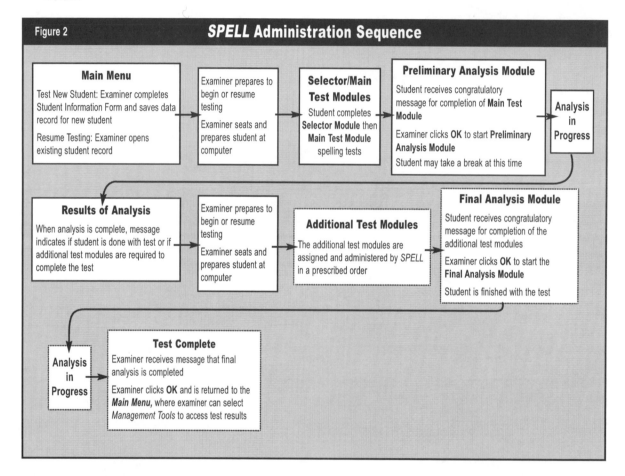

Figure 2 — **SPELL Administration Sequence**

Main Menu

Test New Student: Examiner completes Student Information Form and saves data record for new student

Resume Testing: Examiner opens existing student record

Examiner prepares to begin or resume testing

Examiner seats and prepares student at computer

Selector/Main Test Modules

Student completes **Selector Module** then **Main Test Module** spelling tests

Preliminary Analysis Module

Student receives congratulatory message for completion of **Main Test Module**

Examiner clicks **OK** to start **Preliminary Analysis Module**

Student may take a break at this time

Analysis in Progress

Results of Analysis

When analysis is complete, message indicates if student is done with test or if additional test modules are required to complete the test

Examiner prepares to begin or resume testing

Examiner seats and prepares student at computer

Additional Test Modules

The additional test modules are assigned and administered by *SPELL* in a prescribed order

Final Analysis Module

Student receives congratulatory message for completion of the additional test modules

Examiner clicks **OK** to start the **Final Analysis Module**

Student is finished with the test

Analysis in Progress

Test Complete

Examiner receives message that final analysis is completed

Examiner clicks **OK** and is returned to the *Main Menu,* where examiner can select *Management Tools* to access test results

Selector Module

The **Selector Module** is used to determine the most appropriate level of the **Main Test Module** to administer to an individual student. All students must complete the **Selector Module.**

Approximate Testing Time

The testing time is typically between 3 and 5 minutes. The length may vary, depending on the number of items presented for the individual student and the student's own pace.

Instructions

The character guide—either Fiona or Quinn—welcomes the student, explains the purpose of the task, and gives the student specific instructions for completing the task (see page 66). For each item, Fiona or Quinn prompts the student to spell a word by requesting the student's attention (e.g., "Here we go..." or "Listen...") and then presenting the target word in isolation, in a sentence, and again in isolation (e.g., "Cat. The cat chased the mouse. Cat").

Practice Items

Three practice items are presented using the format described above. The student uses the keyboard to type his or her spelling of each practice word, with simultaneous display of each typed response onscreen, and then uses a mouse to click **OK** to proceed to the next practice item.

If the student does not respond within 10 seconds, the computer will repeat the practice item one time. The student may also request replay of the practice item by clicking **Repeat.** There is no limit on the number of requested repetitions for the practice items. Corrective feedback from the character guide is provided for the practice items.

The character guide alerts the student when the practice items have been completed and the first part of the test is about to begin. The student is instructed to click **OK** when ready to begin the test items.

Test Items

Test items are presented in the same format as practice items. The word to be spelled is presented verbally and the student uses the keyboard to type his or her spelling of each test word, with simultaneous display of each typed response onscreen, and then uses a mouse to click **OK** to proceed to the next test item. (For a complete list of test items for the **Selector Module**, see Appendix H.)

The number of items and the specific items presented will vary, based on the student's grade and spelling grade level entered on the Student Information Form and the student's accuracy of performance on the **Selector Module** items.

Selector Module: Instructions from Fiona

Selector Module: Instructions from Quinn

Main Test Module

The **Main Test Module** is used to collect a sample of the student's spelling of between 82 and 184 words for analysis. There are four levels of the **Main Test Module,** and the level of assessment most appropriate for the individual student is determined by the student's performance on the **Selector Module** items. All students must complete the **Main Test Module.**

Approximate Testing Time

SPELL is an untimed test. The testing times in Table 3 are estimates only and will vary from student to student depending on the student's own pace.

Instructions

The character guide—either Fiona or Quinn—congratulates the student on finishing the first part of the test and tells the student that it is time to begin the second part of the test. The guide prompts the student to spell a word by requesting the student's attention and then presenting the target word in isolation, in a sentence, and again in isolation (e.g., "Listen…. Chain. The chain fell off my bike. Chain").

Practice Items

No practice items are presented.

Test Items

The student uses the keyboard to type his or her spelling of each test word (see page 68), with simultaneous display of each typed response onscreen, and then clicks **OK** to proceed to the next test item. (For a complete list of test items for the **Main Test Module** Levels 1, 2, 3, and 4, see Appendices I, J, K, and L, respectively.) If the student does not respond within 10 seconds,

Table 3

MAIN TEST MODULE TESTING ESTIMATES

Level	Number of Test Items	Approximate Testing Time
1	82	30–40 minutes
2	141	35–45 minutes
3	179	45–60 minutes
4	184	45–60 minutes

Main Test Module: Test Item Screen

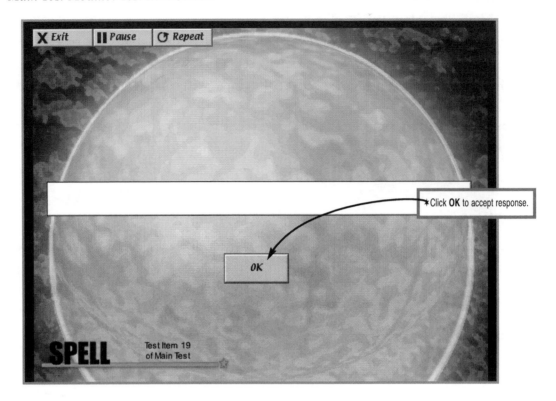

Main Test Module: Test Item Response

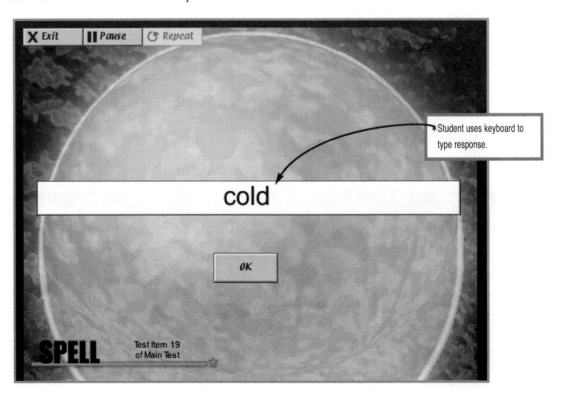

the computer will repeat the test item one time. The student may also request replay of the test item by clicking **Repeat.** Only one repetition is allowed and no corrective feedback is provided by the character guide for the test items.

Additional Test Modules

SPELL offers six additional test modules to gather further information after a student completes the **Main Test Module.** Each of these additional modules targets a specific skill area (see Table 4) complete analysis of a student's spelling errors. The **Spell Book Modules** may be presented only when Level 3 or Level 4 of the **Main Test Module** has been administered.

Will-O-Wisp I

This module is administered only if information about the student's phoneme segmentation skills is needed to complete analysis of the student's spelling errors in the **Main Test Module.** Students who completed Levels 1, 2, 3, or 4 of the **Main Test Module** may be required to complete this additional test module.

Approximate Testing Time
The testing time is typically between 3 and 5 minutes. The length may vary, depending on the number of items presented for the individual student and the student's own pace.

Instructions
Fiona or Quinn introduces the student to the setting for the **Will-O-Wisp I Module.** The Will-O-Wisp then appears onscreen and provides the student with specific instructions for completing the task (see page 71).

Practice Items
The Will-O-Wisp requests the student's attention and prompts the student to click on him (represented by the magical orb) once for each sound he or she hears in a given word. Five practice items are presented using the format described above. The student uses the mouse to click on the orb (once for each sound in the word) and then clicks anywhere on the water to signal the completion of his or her response. If the student does not respond within 10 seconds, the computer will repeat the practice item one time. The student may also request replay of the practice item by clicking **Repeat.** There is no limit on the number of requested repetitions of the practice items. Corrective feedback from the Will-O-Wisp is provided for the practice items.

Test Items
The Will-O-Wisp alerts the student when presentation of the test items is about to begin. The specific test items presented and the number of items presented will vary, based on the student's performance in the **Main Test Module.** The student uses the mouse to click on the orb (once

for each sound in the word) and then clicks anywhere on the water to signal the completion of his or her response. If the student does not respond within 10 seconds, the computer will repeat the test item one time. The student may also request replay of the test item by clicking **Repeat.** Only one repetition is allowed and no corrective feedback is provided by the Will-O-Wisp for the test items. An animation is presented to signal the completion of the **Will-O-Wisp I Module.**

Will-O-Wisp II

This module is administered only if information about the student's syllable segmentation skills is needed to complete analysis of the student's spelling errors in the **Main Test Module.** Students who completed Levels 1, 2, 3, or 4 of the **Main Test Module** may be required to complete this additional test module.

Approximate Testing Time

The testing time is typically between 3 and 5 minutes. The length may vary, depending on the number of items presented for the individual student and the student's own pace.

Instructions

Fiona or Quinn introduces the student to the setting for the **Will-O-Wisp II Module.** The Will-O-Wisp then appears onscreen and provides the student with specific instructions for completing the task (see page 71).

Practice Items

The Will-O-Wisp requests the student's attention and prompts the student to click on him (represented by the magical orb) once for each syllable he or she hears in a given word.

Will-O-Wisp I and Will-O-Wisp II: Instructions from the Will-O-Wisp

Three practice items are presented using the format described above. The student uses the mouse to click on the orb (once for each syllable in the word) and then clicks anywhere on the water to signal the completion of his or her response. If the student does not respond within 10 seconds, the computer will repeat the practice item one time. The student may also request replay of the practice item by clicking **Repeat.** There is no limit on the number of requested repetitions of the practice items. Corrective feedback from the Will-O-Wisp is provided for the practice items.

Test Items

The Will-O-Wisp alerts the student when presentation of the test items is about to begin. The specific test items presented and the number of items presented will vary, based on the student's performance in the **Main Test Module.** The student uses the mouse to click on the orb (once for each syllable in the word) and then clicks anywhere on the water to signal the completion of his or her response. If the student does not respond within 10 seconds, the computer will repeat the test item one time. The student may also request replay of the test item by clicking **Repeat.** Only one repetition is allowed and no corrective feedback is provided by the Will-O-Wisp for the test items. An animation is presented to signal the completion of the **Will-O-Wisp II Module.**

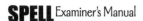

Magical Pond I

This module is administered only if information about the student's ability to phonemically discriminate vowels is needed to complete analysis of the student's spelling errors in the **Main Test Module.** Students who completed Levels 1, 2, 3, or 4 of the **Main Test Module** may be required to complete this additional test module.

Approximate Testing Time

The testing is typically between 3 and 12 minutes. the length may vary, depending on the number of items presented for the individual student and the student's own pace.

Instructions

Fiona or Quinn introduces the student to the setting for the **Magical Pond I Module.** The Will-O-Wisp then appears onscreen and provides the student with specific instructions for completing the task (see page 74).

Practice Items

The Will-O-Wisp requests the student's attention and prompts the student to listen as a word is repeated over and over and to click on him (represented by the magical orb) when he or she hears a different word (e.g., "back-back-back-back-back-back-bake"). Four practice items are presented using the format described above. The student uses the mouse to click on the orb when he or she hears a change to a different word (i.e., *bake).* Unlike the other modules, neither **Magical Pond Module** allows students to have the practice items repeated. Corrective feedback is provided for the practice items.

Test Items

The Will-O-Wisp alerts the student when presentation of the test items is about to begin. The specific test items presented and the number of items presented will vary, based on the student's performance in the **Main Test Module.** The student uses the mouse to click on the orb when he or she hears a change to a different word. Unlike the other modules, neither **Magical Pond Module** allows students to have the test items repeated. No corrective feedback is provided by the Will-O-Wisp for the test items. An animation is presented to signal the completion of the **Magical Pond I Module.**

Magical Pond II

This module is administered only if information about the student's ability to phonemically discriminate vowels and liquids is needed to complete analysis of the student's spelling errors in the **Main Test Module.** Only students who completed Levels 2, 3, or 4 of the **Main Test Module** may be required to complete this additional test module.

Approximate Testing Time

The testing time is typically between 3 and 12 minutes. The length may vary, depending on the number of items presented for the individual student and the student's own pace.

Instructions

Fiona or Quinn introduces the student to the setting for the **Magical Pond II Module.** The Will-O-Wisp then appears onscreen and provides the student with specific instructions for completing the task (see below).

Practice Items

The Will-O-Wisp requests the student's attention and prompts the student to listen as a word is repeated over and over and to click on him (represented by the magical orb) when he or she hears different word (e.g., "fur-fur-fur-fur-fur-fuh"). Four practice items are presented using the format described above. The student uses the mouse to click on the orb when he or she hears a change to a different word (i.e., *fuh)*. Unlike the other modules, neither **Magical Pond Module** allows students to have the practice items repeated. Corrective feedback from the Will-O-Wisp is provided for the practice items.

Test Items

The Will-O-Wisp alerts the student when presentation of the test items is about to begin. The specific test items presented and the number of items presented will vary, based on the student's performance in the **Main Test Module.** The student uses the mouse to click on the orb when he or she hears a change to a different word. Unlike the other modules, neither **Magical Pond Module** allows students to have the practice items repeated. No corrective feedback is provided by the Will-O-Wisp for the test items. An animation is presented to signal the completion of the **Magical Pond II Module.**

Magical Pond I and Magical Pond II: Instructions from the Will-O-Wisp

Spell Book I

This module is administered only if information about the student's ability to spell specific uninflected and underived words is needed to complete analysis of the student's spelling errors in the **Main Test Module.** Only students who completed Level 3 or 4 of the **Main Test Module** may be required to complete this additional test module.

Approximate Testing Time

The testing time is typically between 3 and 12 minutes. The length may vary, depending on the number of items presented for the individual student and the student's own pace.

Instructions

Fiona or Quinn appears onscreen and introduces the student to the setting for the **Spell Book I Module.** The character guide then provides the student with specific instructions for completing the task (see page 75).

Practice Items

The character guide requests the student's attention and prompts the student to spell a word presented in isolation, in a sentence, and again in isolation (e.g., "Listen.... Desk. A student sits at a desk. Desk"). Three practice items are presented using the format described above. The student uses the keyboard to type his or her spelling of each practice word, with simultaneous display of each typed response onscreen, and then uses a mouse to click **OK** to proceed to the next practice item. If the student does not respond within 10 seconds, the computer will repeat the practice item one time. The student may also request replay of the practice item by clicking **Repeat.** There is no limit on the number of requested repetitions of the practice items. Corrective feedback from the character guide is provided for the practice items.

Test Items

Fiona or Quinn alerts the student when presentation of the test items is about to begin. The specific test items presented and the number of items presented will vary, based on the student's performance in the **Main Test Module.** The student uses the keyboard to type his or her spelling of each test word, with simultaneous display of each typed response onscreen, and then uses a mouse to click **OK** to proceed to the next test item. If the student does not respond within 10 seconds, the computer will repeat the test item one time. The student may also request replay of the test item by clicking **Repeat.** Only one repetition is allowed and no corrective feedback is provided by the character guide for the test items. A graphical animation is presented to signal the completion of the **Spell Book I Module.**

Spell Book I and Spell Book II: Instructions from Fiona

Spell Book I: Practice Screen

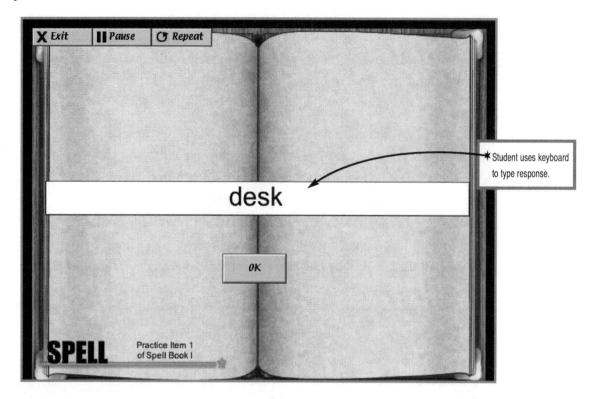

Spell Book II

This module is administered only if information about the student's morphological knowledge is needed to complete analysis of the student's spelling errors in the **Main Test Module.** Only students who completed Level 3 or 4 of the **Main Test Module** may be required to complete this additional test module.

Approximate Testing Time

The testing time is typically between 3 and 12 minutes. The length may vary, depending on the number of items presented for the individual student and the student's own pace.

Instructions

Fiona or Quinn introduces the student to the setting for the **Spell Book II Module.** The character guide then appears onscreen and provides the student with specific instructions for completing the task.

Practice Items

The character guide requests the student's attention and prompts the student to complete a sentence by typing a word that is related to a word presented before a sentence (e.g., "Musician. He likes to play _____"). Three practice items are presented using the format described above. The student uses the keyboard to type his or her spelling of each practice word, with simultaneous display of each typed response onscreen, and then clicks OK to proceed to the next practice item. If the student does not respond within 10 seconds, the computer will repeat the practice item one time. The student may also request replay of the practice item by clicking **Repeat.** There is no limit on the number of requested repetitions of the practice items. Corrective feedback from the character guide is provided for the practice items.

Test Items

Fiona or Quinn alerts the student when presentation of the test items is about to begin. The specific test items presented and the number of items presented will vary, based on the student's performance in the **Main Test Module.** The student uses the keyboard to type his or her spelling of each test word, with simultaneous display of each typed response onscreen, and then uses a mouse to click **OK** to proceed to the next test item. If the student does not respond within 10 seconds, the computer will repeat the test item one time. The student may also request replay of the test item by clicking **Repeat.** Only one repetition is allowed and no corrective feedback is provided by the character guide for the test items. A graphical animation is presented to signal the completion of the **Spell Book II Module.**

Spell Book I and II: Instructions from Quinn

Spell Book II: Practice Screen

Administration Checklist

The following checklist has been created to assist the examiner in properly administering *SPELL*.

Before Administration

☐ Review Part I and Part II of the *Examiner's Manual*.

☐ Install the software and create a password.

☐ Click on the *Examiner Preview* folder tab to review the software.

☐ Gather all the student information needed to complete the Student Information Form.

☐ Prepare the environment, equipment (e.g., headphones), and student for testing.

Testing a New Student

☐ Click on the **Test New Student** folder tab.

☐ Complete the Student Information Form.

☐ Sit with the student for practice items and assist as needed.

☐ Visually monitor the student throughout testing.

☐ Provide breaks as needed.

Resume Testing of Student

❑ Click on the **Resume Testing** folder tab.

❑ Select and open the student's data record and verify that the information is correct.

❑ Prepare the student to resume testing.

❑ Visually monitor the student throughout testing.

❑ Provide breaks as needed.

Preliminary Analysis Module

❑ Click **OK** to begin the **Preliminary Analysis Module.**

❑ Wait for the analysis.

❑ Check if the program has indicated if student is finished or if additional test modules are required.

Additional Test Modules

❑ Return the student to the computer and click **OK** to continue testing.

❑ Sit with the student during practice items for each additional test module and assist as needed.

❑ Visually monitor the student throughout testing.

❑ Provide breaks as needed (optimum time for a break is between modules).

Final Analysis Module

❑ Click **OK** to begin the **Final Analysis Module.**

❑ Wait for the analysis.

❑ Access the results by clicking on the *Management Tools* folder tab.

Appendices

Appendix A: Frequently Asked Questions 82

Appendix B: Suggestions for Implementing Spelling Recommendations
           in the Language Arts Curriculum 88

Appendix C: Examples and Definitions of Spelling Terms
           for Parents and Teachers 90

Appendix D: Orthographic Spelling Patterns and Rules 92

Appendix E: Morphological Spelling Patterns and Rules 103

Appendix F: Sample Letter to Parents 112

Appendix G: Sample Letter to Teachers 114

Appendix H: List of Selector Module Test Items 116

Appendix I: List of Level 1 Main Test Module Test Items 118

Appendix J: List of Level 2 Main Test Module Test Items 122

Appendix K: List of Level 3 Main Test Module Test Items 128

Appendix L: List of Level 4 Main Test Module Test Items 135

Frequently Asked Questions

- **Should I administer *SPELL* as part of a diagnostic battery?**

  It is recommended that the examiner administer a standardized spelling test (e.g., Larsen, Hammill, and Moats's [1991] Test of Written Spelling–4) as part of the diagnostic battery to qualify a student for services. Once the student is enrolled in an instructional program, *SPELL* can be administered to pinpoint specific instructional objectives for the individual student. Depending on the amount of time available for testing, the examiner may elect to include *SPELL* as part of a diagnostic battery.

- **Can I administer *SPELL* without the use of headphones?**

  The use of headphones for administration of *SPELL* is highly recommended to maximize validity of test results.

- **What type of headphones is recommended for use with *SPELL?***

  The headphones commonly used for portable audio devices are appropriate for use with *SPELL*.

- **Why does the order of presentation of the Selector Module items vary from student to student?**

  The starting item number for the **Selector Module** is determined by the individual student's grade and spelling grade level as entered by the examiner on the Student Information Form. The specific test items and the order of the test items presented to the student in the **Selector Module** are determined by the individual student's performance in the **Selector Module.** The **Selector Module** presents the items in the order necessary to establish a basal and then a ceiling for the individual student and discontinues the **Selector Module** once a ceiling has been established.

- **How do I know which level of the Main Test Module has been selected for administration to the individual student?**

  The level of the **Main Test Module** selected by *SPELL* for administration to an individual student is indicated in the lower right corner of the student information displayed when student begins and resumes testing in the **Main Test Module.** Next Module: Main Test (L1) denotes Level 1; (L2) denotes Level 2, and so on. After the student has finished spelling the first 20 words of the **Main Test Module,** *SPELL* automatically checks for a minimum spelling accuracy level for selected spelling patterns. If the student does not meet the minimal criterion set by the program, *SPELL* will automatically and seamlessly drop to the next lowest level of the **Main Test Module.**

• **Why does the test item number in the lower left corner of the screen not always correspond to the item number in lists of words for the Selector or Main Test Module contained in the Appendices?**

Because the test item counter in the lower left corner of the screen reflects the number of items completed by the student, there is not always a direct correspondence between the counter number and test item number found in the list of words. This is because the starting test item number for the **Selector Module** is determined by the student's grade and/or spelling grade level and not all students will need to complete all 40 items in the **Selector Module.** Also, a word previously completed in the **Selector Module** will not be presented again in the **Main Test Module.** The examiner can use the number that appears in the lower left corner of the screen to gauge the approximate number of items remaining to be completed in the **Main Test Module.**

• **After I finish testing a student, why can't I locate the student's name under** *Resume Testing?*

Once a student has completed the *SPELL* assessment, his or her name is removed from the list of students displayed under the *Resume Testing* folder tab. For students who have completed *SPELL,* you may access their records under the *Management Tools* folder tab.

• **Does** *SPELL* **accept spellings that contain characters other than the letters of the alphabet?**

The *SPELL* program will accept keyboard input of the 26 letters of the alphabet and apostrophes, hyphens, and periods. Although none of the target words in *SPELL* contains apostrophes, hyphens, or periods, these characters are allowed since they are sometimes used to spell words, as is the case for contractions, possessives, compound words, and abbreviations. *SPELL* does not include apostrophes, hyphens, or periods in its analysis of the student's spellings, but will list the words in which these characters appear on the student's report. The examiner is encouraged to review the list of words for a specific pattern of misuse that may need to be addressed.

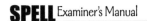

- **Does *SPELL* analyze a student's spelling of homonyms, contractions, possessives, and abbreviations?**

No. Misspelling of these types of words is an easily recognizable error pattern. Not including these types of spelling patterns in *SPELL* helped keep the number of test items and the length of the assessment within a reasonable range. If the student exhibits a pattern of homonym confusion or misspelling of contractions, possessives, and abbreviations, the professional can target this error pattern through development of semantic knowledge and mental orthographic images.

- **Is the student's spelling performance affected by keyboard response?**

There is evidence that a student's spelling performance is not affected by using keyboard input for spelling response (Beggs, Schofield, Masterson, & Apel, 2001). The accuracy of children's spellings entered via a keyboard versus pencil and paper was compared in students in Grades 2–6. Although the pencil-and-paper spellings were slightly better for the children in Grade 2, there were no differences in the other grades, with the exception of the fourth graders, who actually performed better when using a keyboard. Of particular interest was the finding that the children's spelling accuracy in the two modes was not influenced by keyboarding proficiency (measured as words per minute).

- **What criteria were used to select root words for assessing morphological knowledge of the relationship between base words and inflected and derived forms?**

In most cases, the root word was determined by the etymology of the inflected or derived form. In some cases, however, the etymological root was judged to have limited semantic value. In other words, the likelihood that individuals would utilize the etymological root to identify a semantic relationship with the derived form was judged to be minimal. For example, many individuals would not consider *import* as related to *importance* but would consider *important* to be related to *importance*. In these cases, a more familiar form of the word, which could be used to aid the spelling of a second derived form, was selected based on systematic examination of the test items to determine the strength of the semantic relationship to the derived form.

- **How was familiarity of vocabulary controlled for in selection of the test items?**

Content validity measures were implemented to select test items that were within the vocabulary level for individuals who would most likely receive a particular level of assessment.

- **Does *SPELL* exhaustively test every spelling pattern of English?**

The construction of any test must balance the desire to assess the target skill or skills in every possible context with the practical constraints of creating a test that can be completed within a reasonable amount of time. *SPELL* assesses over 120 of the most common spelling patterns. The decision about which spelling patterns to include was based on several published resources as well as clinical judgment by the authors about what patterns were most important to include.

- **Is normative data available for *SPELL?***

SPELL is a prescriptive assessment tool; that is, *SPELL* identifies error patterns and makes specific recommendations for spelling intervention. Normative data are not required for a prescriptive assessment tool. Standardized tests quantify a student's performance relative to a population of peers. Professionals should keep in mind that standardized tools do not allow a clinician to determine goals, whereas this prescriptive tool does

- **What type of field-testing was conducted in the development of *SPELL*?**

Hundreds of spelling samples were collected from individuals ages 7 through adult. These spellings samples were used to assess the performance accuracy of all the components of the *SPELL* software. The collected data were hand-scored and analyzed by a speech-language pathologist experienced in the diagnosis and remediation of spelling. The same data were also analyzed by the *SPELL* software program. The results of the human evaluation were then compared with the results from the *SPELL* program to assess *SPELL*'s accuracy of performance. If any discrepancies were identified, the source of the discrepancy was investigated, identified, and corrected. The final analyses revealed *SPELL*'s accuracy of performance to be 98% versus the human clinician's accuracy of performance of 75%.

- **Can I use the Selector Module to determine if the student is within normal limits and whether the student requires administration of the full assessment?**

SPELL does not provide a normative measure of a student's spelling skills and cannot be used to determine if a student's spelling ability is within normal limits. The domain of English spelling is massive, which makes it impractical to sample every potential orthographic pattern. The **Selector Module** probes the student's spelling of various spelling patterns to determine the most appropriate patterns (i.e., the most appropriate level of *SPELL)*

to use to fully assess in an individual student. Because spelling development is an ongoing process, all individuals with some amount of misspellings could benefit from a full *SPELL* assessment. It is left to the examiner's discretion to determine whether to invest the time required for completion of a full *SPELL* assessment.

- **How often should I re-administer *SPELL*?**

Each level of *SPELL* assesses different spelling patterns, with the spelling patterns assessed across Levels 1–4 and organized according to the general developmental sequence of spelling ability. After an initial administration of *SPELL*, and once the student's spelling of targeted patterns has stabilized, it is recommended that *SPELL* be re-administered to document progress and to assess the next set of spelling patterns in the developmental sequence.

- **How might dialect affect spelling performance?**

The effects of dialect on spelling performance are not currently known. There are some anecdotal data to suggest that some individuals who speak a nonstandard form of English may demonstrate differences in spelling that reflect their dialect. Until more is known, it would be wise to consider the characteristics of the individual's dialect to determine whether *SPELL* results reflect the influences of the student's dialect. If this appears to be true, the professional should consider the target spelling patterns to represent differences in spelling rather than a delay or impairment in spelling. A difference in spelling does not, however, preclude facilitating a student's spelling development and correct spelling of targeted patterns using the learning objectives recommended by *SPELL*.

- **How might speech production errors affect spelling performance?**

The limited data available that address this issue suggest that articulation errors do not carry over into spelling. For the children who have been studied, it does not appear that their speech production is represented in their internal representation of the word. It is possible, however, that the spellings of students who are spelling phonetically may be affected by their misarticulation of sounds.

- **How can I export the student reports as an electronic file?**

All *SPELL* reports are saved and accessed within the *SPELL* program. You can export *SPELL* reports in PDF format if you have Adobe Acrobat Writer installed on your computer.

Simply select the Acrobat PDF Writer device in the **Print** dialog box when printing a report to export the report from the *SPELL* program.

• **Why does it take a long time to open a student record?**

The amount of time it takes to open a record is determined by your computer's specifications. If the accessing of student records is sluggish, we recommend that you use *Management Tools* to periodically purge old student records from the student list. Be sure to print and save hard copies of the student's reports before purging the student's data record, as the student's data will be permanently deleted from the *SPELL* program.

For additional FAQs, visit *http://www.learningbydesign.com/faqs/index.htm*.

Suggestions for Implementing Spelling Recommendations in the Language Arts Curriculum

Phonology-Based Spelling Instruction

★ The goal is to foster awareness of sounds in words with the understanding that letters are used to represent sounds in words.

★ Sound out phonetically spelled words and encourage students to sound out the word as they spell; slowly say the word aloud as students spell the word.

Phonics-Based Spelling Instruction

★ The goal is to teach the different letters and letter combinations that can represent a sound.

★ Display the alphabet on the classroom wall; establish key words for alphabetic letters.

★ Encourage letter hunts for all the letters in a list of words that have the same sound.

★ Address phonetic context, syllable and word position constraints on sound-symbol correspondences (e.g., back vs. bake, tick vs. attic, count vs. account).

Pattern and Rule-Based Spelling Instruction

★ The goal is to develop knowledge of letter patterns and rules for combining letters to spell words.

★ The most important rule is Don't teach the rule! Create opportunities for students to discover the pattern themselves and to use their own words to describe the pattern or rule.

★ Contrast the correct spelling of a target pattern with another familiar word (e.g., rate vs. rat). Guide students through explaining how and why the words look different.

★ Teach spelling patterns in a developmental sequence.

★ Address phonetic context, and syllable and word position constraints on spelling patterns.

★ Group weekly spelling words together according to target pattern; add words to the list so that each target pattern is represented by at least three or four words.

★ Provide ample opportunities to practice new spelling patterns in dictated spelling lists and in controlled writing tasks before using the patterns in authentic writing tasks.

Morphology- and Semantics-Based Spelling Instruction

★ The goal is to use the meaning of words and parts of words to spell.

★ Discuss meaning of words and identify relationships between and among words.

★ Teach correct spelling of inflections and derivations along with the meaning of these word parts.

★ Contrast inflected vs. noninflected and derived vs. nonderived word endings (e.g., rocking vs. king, importance vs. dance).

★ Create opportunities for students to discover rules for modifying words when adding prefixes and suffixes.

★ Teach transparent derived words before teaching semitransparent or opaque derived words.

Mental Orthographic Image-Based Spelling Instruction

★ The goal is to develop clear and complete mental images of words in long-term memory.

★ Always encourage students to print the word rather than recite the word's spelling.

★ Discuss characteristics of the printed word; visualize the word.

★ Present intentional misspellings for correction by students; encourage students' self-monitoring and proofing of their own work.

★ Encourage students with poor penmanship to use a word processor for their writing work.

Examples and Definitions of Spelling Terms for Parents and Teachers

★ PHONOLOGY-BASED SPELLING INSTRUCTION: Spelling instruction that fosters awareness of sounds in words with the understanding that letters are used to represent sounds in words.

★ PHONICS-BASED SPELLING INSTRUCTION: Spelling instruction that focuses on teaching the different letters and letter combinations that can represent a sound.

★ PATTERN AND RULE-BASED SPELLING INSTRUCTION: Spelling instruction that focuses on developing knowledge of letter patterns and rules for combining letters to spell words.

★ SEMANTICS AND MORPHOLOGY-BASED SPELLING INSTRUCTION: Spelling instruction that focuses on understanding and using the meaning of words and parts of words to spell words correctly.

★ MENTAL ORTHOGRAPHIC IMAGE-BASED SPELLING INSTRUCTION: Spelling instruction that focuses on developing clear and complete mental images of words in long-term memory to spell words correctly.

★ ABUTTING CONSONANTS: Adjacent consonants that do not form a blend (e.g., ct in collect).

★ NASAL CLUSTER: A combination of two or three adjacent consonants within the same syllable and including m, n, or ng (e.g., champ, hand, jungle).

★ LIQUID CLUSTER: A combination of two or three adjacent consonants within the same syllable and including r or l (e.g., cross, splash).

★ CONDITIONING SILENT E: A silent e that causes the preceding consonant to be a soft consonant (e.g., lace, page).

★ NONCONDITIONING SILENT E: A silent e that does not affect the pronunciation of the preceding consonant (e.g., like, cape).

★ IRREGULAR PAST TENSE VERBS: A past tense verb that does not follow conventional spelling rules (e.g., caught).

★ INFLECTED WORDS: Verbs that end with -ed, -ing (e.g., walked, swimming) and verbs and plural nouns that end with -s, -es (e.g., walks, cats, washes, dishes).

★ DERIVED WORDS: Words that begin with a prefix (e.g., disallow) or end with a suffix (e.g., investment) and the prefix or suffix changes the word's class (e.g., teach [verb] vs. teacher [noun]) or the word's meaning (e.g., correct vs. incorrect).

★ **Derived Words with Both Orthographic and Phonological Transparency:** Words for which the addition of a prefix or suffix does not change the pronunciation or the spelling of the base word (e.g., correct → incorrect).

★ **Derived Words with Orthographic Transparency Only:** Words for which the addition of a prefix or suffix changes the pronunciation of the base word but does not change the spelling of the base word (e.g., magic → magician).

★ **Derived Words with Phonological Transparency Only:** Words for which the addition of a prefix or suffix changes the spelling of the base word but does not change the pronunciation of the base word (e.g., penny → penniless).

★ **Opaque Derived Words:** Words for which the addition of a prefix or suffix changes both the spelling and the pronunciation of the base word (e.g., caution → cautious).

Orthographic Spelling Patterns and Rules

The following lists of orthographic rules for English spelling of base words were compiled from a variety of sources. The lists are comprehensive and, while perhaps not exhaustive, cover the extensive domain of orthographic spelling patterns evaluated by the *SPELL* program. The lists do not include rules that have multiple exceptions, since these spelling patterns are more effectively taught through development of mental orthographic images.

A. Sound-Symbol Correspondences

International Phonetic Alphabet (IPA) symbols are used to represent phonemes in the *SPELL Examiner's Manual*. Because the *SPELL* software does not use IPA symbols, the corresponding letters used in the software are listed in parentheses next to the IPA symbol, when appropriate.

Phoneme	Common Spellings	Example(s)
STOP CONSONANTS		
/p/	p	pig
	pp	apple
/b/	b	bed
	bb	bubble
/t/	t	toy
	tt	little
/d/	d	dog
	dd	daddy
	ld	could
/k/	c	cat
	k	kite
	ck	back
	cc	account
	ch	school
	lk	talk
/g/	g	goat
	gg	wiggle
	gh	ghost
/ɾ/ (flap)	t	city, later
	d	model, ladle
	tt	letter
	dd	ladder

Phoneme	Common Spellings	Example(s)
FRICATIVE CONSONANTS		
/f/	f	fly
	ff	off
	lf	half
	ph	phone
	gh	tough
/v/	v	van
/θ/ (voiceless th)	th	think
/ð/ (voiced th)	th	they
/s/	s	sit
	ss	class
	c	circle
	sc	scene
/z/	z	zoo
	zz	puzzle
	s	use
	ss	scissors
/ʃ/ (sh)	sh	shoe
	s	sugar
	c(i)	social
	ss	tissue
	ss(i)	mission
	ch	chute
	t(i)	mention
/ʒ/ (zh)	s(i)	occasion
	s	measure
	z	azure
	g(e)	beige
/h/	h	he
	wh	who

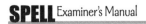

Phoneme	Common Spellings	Example(s)
AFFRICATE CONSONANTS		
/tʃ/ (ch)	ch	chin
	tch	match
	t	nature
	t(i)	question
/dʒ/ (dz)	j	jump
	g	gem
	dg(e)	judge
	d	educate
	d(i)	soldier
	dj	adjourn
	gg	exaggerate
	g(i)	region
NASAL CONSONANTS		
/m/	m	mop
	mm	hammer
	lm	calm
	mb	comb
	mn	hymn
/n/	n	net
	nn	dinner
	gn	gnome
	kn	know
	pn	pneumonia
/ŋ/ (ng)	ng	ring
	n(k), n(g), n(d)	think, jungle, handkerchief
GLIDE CONSONANTS		
/j/	y	yellow
	i(o)	scallion
/w/	w	wet
	wh	when

Phoneme	Common Spellings	Example(s)
LIQUID CONSONANTS		
/r/	r	rug
	rr	hurry
	wr	write
/l/	l	lake
	ll	pill
VOCALIC /l/ & /r/		
/l/	el	camel
	al	signal
	le	little
	il	pencil
	ul	mogul
/ɝ, ɚ/ (vocalic r)	ar	burglar
	er	herd, hammer
	or	world, tumor
	our	journey, glamour
	ure	sure, measure
	ur	church
	yr	martyr
	ear	early
	ir	stir, elixir
SHORT VOWELS		
/æ/	a	bat
/ɛ/	e	bed
	ea	head
	ie	friend
/ɪ/	i	bit
	y	gym
	ui	build
/ɑ/	o	pot
	a	father
	aa	bazaar
/ʌ/	u	cut
	ou	country
	oo	blood

95

Phoneme	Common Spellings	Example(s)
OTHER LAX VOWELS		
/ʊ/	u	put
	oo	foot
	ou	could
/ɔ/	o	cloth
	a	fall
	augh	caught
	aw	saw
	ough	thought
TENSE VOWELS		
/e/	a	able
	ai	rain
	ea	steak
	ay	may
	ey	obey
	eigh	eight
	a_e	make
	ei	beige
/i/	e	me
	ee	see
	ea	pea
	ei	receipt
	eo	people
	ey	key
	ie	relieve
	y	city
	e_e	concede
	i_e	machine
	ie_e	believe
	ei_e	conceive
/o/	o	no
	oa	boat
	ow	low
	oe	toe

	ou	shoulder
	ough	though
	o_e	note
/u, ju/	u	truly, unit
	oo	boot
	o	do
	ew	crew, few
	ou	group
	ue	true, value
	ui	fruit
	ough	through
	u_e	flute, use

VOWEL DIPHTHONGS

/ɑɪ/	i	kind
	ye	bye
	eigh	height
	igh	sigh
	y	my
	uy	buy
	ie	tie
	i_e	bike
	y_e	byte
/ɔɪ/	oi	boil
	oy	toy
/ɑu/	ou	out
	ow	pow
	ough	bough

B. Long vs. Short Vowel Principles

RULE 1: The letter *k* is used to spell /k/ only after long vowels; the letters *ck* and *c* are used to spell /k/ only after short/lax vowels.

take vs. tack   joke vs. jock   make vs. tarmac

97

Continued on next page

RULE 2: Consonant letters are never doubled after long vowels.

humor vs. hummer   pile vs. pill   liter vs. letter

RULE 3: Consonant letters are always doubled after a short/lax vowel to spell /p, b, n, m, f, s, l, r/ within a word.

| happy | rubber | nanny | hammer |
| traffic | messy | pillow | sorrow |

RULE 4: Consonant letters are almost always doubled after a short/lax vowel to spell /s, f, l/ at the end of a word.

mess   cliff   pill

RULE 5: Consonant letters are always doubled after a short vowel when followed by syllabic *l* spelled with the letters *le*.

paddle   pebble   bottle

RULE 6: The letters *tch* are never used to spell /ʧ/ after long vowels.

reach vs. retch   broach vs. botch

RULE 7: The letters *dge* are used to spell /ʤ/ after short vowels and the letter *g* is used to spell /ʤ/ after long vowels.

judge vs. huge   badge vs. rage

RULE 8: In a closed CVC(C) syllable, a single vowel letter always spells a short vowel. (C = consonant letter, V = vowel letter).

pin vs. pine   can vs. cane

RULE 9: In a closed CVC(C)e syllable, a single vowel letter always spells a long vowel.

tone vs. ton   chute vs. shut

RULE 10: The letters *lk* spell /k/ and the letters *ld* spell /d/ at the end of a word only after a short/lax vowel.

talk   should

RULE 11: The letters *lf, ph, gh* spell /f/ only after a short/lax vowel.

half   graph   tough

RULE 12: The letters *lm, mn* spell /m/ only after a short/lax vowel.

calm   hymn

RULE 13: The letters *gn* spell /n/ only after a long vowel.

reign`   sign

C. Syllable, Word Position, & Phonetic Constraints* on Spelling Patterns**

RULE 1: The letters *ck* are used to spell /k/ at the end of a one syllable word after a short vowel; the letter *c* is used to spell /k/ at the end of a multisyllabic word after a short vowel.

tick vs. attic   rock vs. mystic

RULE 2: When spelling /k/ at the beginning or in the middle of a word, use the letter *c* before the vowel letters *a, o, u* and use the letter *k* before the vowel letters *i, e, y*.

cat   cot   cut   kiss

keg   sky

RULE 3: When spelling /g/ at the beginning or in the middle of a word, use the letter *g* before the vowel letters *a, o, u* and use the letters *gu* before the vowel letters *i, e*.

gate   got   gun   guide

guest

RULE 4: The letters *tch* are always used to spell /tʃ/ after short vowel *a* in single-syllable words.

catch   match

Vowel context is one type of phonetic constraint. Due to the importance and frequency of occurrence of long vs. short vowel constraints, this phonetic constraint is addressed separately in the preceding section: "Long vs. Short Vowel Principles."

**Due to the large number of phonetic contexts in which a sound may occur, SPELL does not systematically assess each of the phonetic constraint rules. The examiner will want to review the lists of words misspelled by a student, and possibly probe with additional words, to glean information about the student's knowledge and use of various phonetic constraint rules.*

D. Word Position Constraints* for Common Spellings of Consonants**

Phoneme	Initial	Medial (Intervocalic)	Final (Including VCe)
STOP CONSONANTS			
/p/	p (pin)	p (open) pp (apple)	p (chip, ripe)
/b/	b (bat)	b (ruby) bb (rubber)	b (crib, tribe)
/t/	t (top)	t (baton) tt (attack)	t (quit, quite)
/d/	d (dog)	d (cadet) dd (daddy)	d (sad) ld (should)
/ɾ/ (flap)	—	tt (latter) t (petal) dd (ladder) d (pedal)	—
/k/	c (coat) k (kite) ch (chord)	c (bacon) k (cookie) cc (account) ch (echo) ck (wacky)	k (make, brook) ck (back) lk (talk) c (comic)
/g/	g (go) gh (ghost)	g (ago) gg (wiggle) gh (aghast)	g (big)
FRICATIVE CONSONANTS			
/f/	f (fish) ph (phone)	f (rifle) ff (office) ph (elephant)	f (knife) ff (cliff) lf (calf) ph (graph) gh (tough)
/v/	v (van)	v (even)	v (have)
/θ/ (voiceless th)	th (think)	th (author)	th (with)
/ð/ (voiced th)	th (they)	th (other)	th (bathe)

/s/	s (sit)	s (aside)	s (case)
	c (cent)	ss (lesson)	ss (class)
	sc (scene)	c (deceit)	c (place)
		sc (muscle)	
/z/	z (zoo)	z (hazel)	z (breeze)
		zz (sizzle)	zz (fuzz)
		s (music)	s (muse)
		ss (scissors)	
/ʃ/ (sh)	sh (shoe)	sh (bishop)	sh (mash)
	s (sugar)	c (glacier)	
	ch (chute)	ss (tissue, mission)	
		ch (machine)	
		t (lotion)	
/ʒ/ (zh)	-–	s (measure, vision)	g (beige)
		z (azure)	
h	h (he)	h (ahead)	–

AFFRICATE CONSONANTS

/tʃ/ (ch)	ch (chin)	ch (achieve)	ch (each)
		tch (hatchet)	tch (match)
		t (nature, question)	
/dʒ/ (dz)	j (jump)	j (ajar)	g (huge)
	g (gem)	g (agent, region)	dg (badge)
		d (education, soldier)	
		dj (adjourn)	
		gg (exaggerate)	

NASAL CONSONANTS

/m/	m (man)	m (camel)	m (crime)
		mm (hammer)	lm (calm)
			mb (comb)
			mn (hymn)
/n/	n (no)	n (many)	n (pin)
	gn (gnome)	nn (penny)	gn (sign)
	kn (know)		
	pn (pneumonia)		
/ŋ/	–	ng, nd, ng (think, handkerchief, jungle)	ng (thing)

GLIDE CONSONANTS			
/j/	y (yellow)	i (scallion)	–
/w/	w (wet) wh (when)	w (away) wh (awhile)	–

LIQUID CONSONANTS			
/r/	r (run) wr (wrong)	r (arise) rr (arrow)	r (fire) rr (purr)
/l/	l (light)	l (elite) ll (yellow)	ll (fill) l (pile)

Positional constraints are for base words only.

**There is limited information available about word position constraints on spellings of nonconsonants. Note that consonants are sometimes conditioned by the following vowel.*

E. Semantic (Word Meaning) Constraints on Spelling Patterns

RULE 1: Always use the letters *wh* to spell /w, hw/ at the beginning of a question word.

what   when   where   why

RULE 2: Always use the letters *wh* to spell /h/ at the beginning of a question word.

who   whom   whose

RULE 3: The letters *ed* spell /t/ or /d/ only when used to spell the past tense inflection.

walked   banged

F. Rule for Conditioning Silent *E*

RULE 1: The letter *e* is required at the end of a word when the absence of the silent *e* would cause the final consonant to change from a soft sound (fricative or affricate) to hard sound (stop) or from a voiceless to voiced sound.

twice   fudge   fuse

Morphological Spelling Patterns and Rules

The following lists of morphological rules for English spelling of inflected and derived words were compiled from a variety of sources in the References list. The lists of rules are comprehensive and, while perhaps not exhaustive, cover the extensive domain of morphological spelling patterns evaluated by the *SPELL* program. The lists do not include rules that have multiple exceptions, since these spelling patterns are more effectively taught through development of mental orthographic images.

I. Inflected Words

A. Rules for Spelling Inflections: Plurals

RULE 1: For most nouns, including base words ending in *e*, add -*s* to form the plural.

cat + s = cats   house + s = houses

flower + s = flowers

RULE 2: For nouns ending in *s*, *ss*, *sh*, *soft ch*, *x* and *zz*, add -*es* to form the plural.

bus + es = buses   church + es = churches

class + es = classes   box + es = boxes

fish + es = fishes   buzz + es = buzzes

RULE 3: When a vowel precedes final *o*, the plural is formed by adding -*s*.

radio + s = radios   rodeo + s = rodeos

RULE 4: When a vowel precedes final *y*, the plural is formed by adding -*s*.

boy + s = boys   day + s = days

monkey + s = monkeys

B. Rules for Modifying Base Words When Spelling Plural Forms

RULE 1: For nouns ending with a consonant + *y*, change *y* to *i* and add -*es* to form the plural.

city → cities   spy → spies

berry → berries

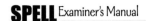

RULE 2: For nouns ending with *f*, change *f* to *v*, and add *-es* to form the plural; when a noun ends in *fe*, the plural is formed by changing *fe* to *ve*, and adding *-s*.

leaf → leaves	thief → thieves
elf → elves	shelf → shelves
knife → knives	life → lives

C. Rules for Spelling Inflections: Regular Verb Forms

RULE 1: When a vowel precedes final *y*, add *-s, -ed, -ing* to form third person present tense, past tense, and present progressive verb forms.

annoy → annoys	employ → employed
deploy → deploying	

RULE 2: When a consonant precedes final *y*, add *-ing* to form present progressive verb forms.

marry → marrying	tally → tallying

RULE 3: For words ending with a long vowel followed by a consonant letter, add *-s, -ed, -ing* to form third person present tense, past tense, and present progressive verb forms.

rain → rains	snow → snowed
fuel → fueling	

RULE 4: For words ending with the long vowel VCe pattern, simply add *-s* to form the third person present tense.

rides → rides	rake → rakes

RULE 5: For words ending with a short vowel followed by a double consonant, add *-s, -ed, -ing* to form third person present tense, past tense, and present progressive verb forms.

dress → dresses	spill → spilled
cuff → cuffing	

RULE 6: For words ending with a short vowel followed by more than one consonant, add *-s, -ed, -ing* to form third person present tense, past tense, and present progressive verb forms.

kick → kicks	blast → blasted
hold → holding	

RULE 7: For words ending with unstressed vocalic *r* or *l,* add *-s, -ed* to form third person present tense and past tense verb forms.

baffle → baffles   cater → catered

RULE 8: For words ending with unstressed vocalic *r,* add *-ing* to form the present progressive verb form.

cater → catering

RULE 9: For words ending in *oe or ee,* add *-s, -ing* to form third person present tense and present progressive verb forms.

shoe → shoes   see → sees

canoe → canoeing   agree → agreeing

RULE 10: For words ending in *ye,* add *-s, -ing* to form the third person present tense and present progressive verb forms.

dye → dyes   eye → eyeing

D. Rules for Modifying Base Words When Spelling Regular Verb Forms

RULE 1: For verbs ending with the short vowel VC pattern, double the final consonant before adding *-ed, -ing* to form past tense and present progressive verb forms.

sip → sipped   omit → omitted

tap → tapping   forget → forgetting

RULE 2: When a consonant precedes final *y,* change *y* to *i* and add *-ed, -es* to form past tense and third person present tense verb forms.

marry → married   tally → tallies

RULE 3: When a verb ends in a hard *c* sound, change *c* to *ck* before adding *-ed, -ing* to maintain the hard *c* sound when forming past tense and present progressive verb forms.

panic → panicked   picnic → picnicking

RULE 4: For verbs ending with the long vowel CVe pattern, drop the final silent *e* before adding *-ed, -ing* to form present progressive and past tense verb forms.

bore → bored   bake → baking

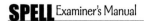

RULE 5: For verbs ending in *oe, ue,* drop the final *e* before adding *-ed, -ing* to form past tense and present progressive verb forms.

hoe → hoed   canoe → canoeing

argue → argued   continue → continuing

RULE 6: For verbs ending in *ye,* drop the final *e* before adding *-ed* to form past tense verb forms.

dye → dyed   eye → eyed

RULE 7: For verbs ending with unstressed vocalic *l* spelled *le,* drop *e* before adding *-ed, -ing* to form past tense and present progressive verb forms.

shuffle → shuffled   rattle → rattled

baffle → baffling   whistle → whistling

RULE 8: When a verb of more than one syllable ends in a single vowel and a single consonant and has the accent on the final syllable, double the final consonant before adding a verb suffix beginning with a vowel.

commit → committed   recur → recurring

II. Derived Words

A. Rules for Spelling Derivational Morphemes: Suffixes

RULE 1: The suffixes *-ty, -ity,* and *-ness* change adjectives into noun forms that mean "the state or condition of being."

cruel → cruelty   sudden → suddenness

hardy → hardiness   complex → complexity

RULE 2: The suffixes *-er* and *-or* and sometimes *-ar* change verbs into noun forms that mean "a person who performs the action."

teach → teacher   sail → sailor

beg → beggar

RULE 3: The suffixes *-ance* and *-ence* change verbs into noun forms that mean "the act of" or "the state of being."

resist → resistance   occur → occurrence

insure → insurance

RULE 4: The suffixes *-ion, -tion, -sion,* and *-ation* change verbs into noun forms that mean "the act of" or "the state of being."

separate → separation   admire → admiration

expand → expansion

RULE 5: The suffixes *-ist, -ian* and *-ician* can be added to some nouns to form a different noun meaning "the person who does, works with, or is skilled at."

piano → pianist   library → librarian

beauty → beautician

RULE 6: The suffix *-al* is used to change many nouns into adjective forms. The suffix *-ial* is used when the *i* is required to condition the final consonant of the base word.

accident → accidental   confidence → confidential

RULE 7: The suffixes *-ary* and *-ory* change nouns and verbs into nouns or adjectives meaning "that which, one who, place where, or pertaining to."

satisfy → satisfactory   custom → customary

RULE 8: The suffix *-ly* is usually added to change an adjectives and nouns into an adverb form.

actual → actually   merry → merrily

RULE 9: The suffix *-y* is usually added to change a verb or noun into an adjective form.

stick → sticky   fish → fishy

RULE 10: The suffixes *-ent* and *-ant* change verbs into adjective or noun forms meaning "one who is or does, that which is or does, or the state of being."

depend → dependent   urge → urgent

serve → servant

RULE 11: The suffixes *-san* and *-zen* change nouns into noun forms meaning "one who belongs to, is a member of."

party → partisan   city → citizen

RULE 12: The suffix *-ment* changes verbs into noun forms meaning "the state or condition resulting from an action, or action or process."

establish → establishment   accomplish → accomplishment

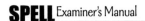

RULE 13: The suffix *-ous* changes nouns into adjective forms meaning "possessing the quality of." The suffix *-ious* is used when the *i* is required to condition the final consonant of the base word.

scandal → scandalous   efficacy → efficacious

RULE 14: The suffixes *-able;* and *-ible* change verbs into noun forms meaning "capable of, fit for, or worthy of."

comfort → comfortable   access → accessible

RULE 15: The suffix *-ure* changes verbs into noun forms meaning "act or process."

fail → failure   catch → capture

RULE 16: The suffix *-ful* changes verbs into adjective forms meaning "full of, character-ized by."

help → helpful   care → careful

RULE 17: The suffix *-cy* changes adjectives into nouns forms meaning "action, practice, state or quality."

decent → decency   discrepant → discrepancy

RULE 18: The suffix *-less* changes nouns into adjective forms meaning "not having, unable to be acted on or to act."

sense → senseless   harm → harmless

RULE 19: The suffix *-ify* changes adjectives into verbs forms meaning "make, form into; invest with the attributes of, make similar to."

clear → clarify   just → justify

RULE 20: The suffix *-ize* changes nouns and adjectives into verbs forms meaning "cause to be or conform to or resemble; to become like."

personal → personalize   victim → victimize

RULE 21: The suffix *-ive* changes nouns and verbs into adjective forms meaning "perform or tend toward an action."

recluse → reclusive   assert → assertive

B. Rules for Spelling Derivational Morphemes: Prefixes

RULE 1: The following prefixes all have the meaning of "not": *un-*, *im-*, *in-*, *il-*, *ir-*, *dis-*, *mis-*. Each of these negative prefixes can be used to change a word to its antonym or opposite.

un- is used most often to change meaning of adjectives:

unlikely   unsuitable

un- can also be used to change meaning of form verbs:

unsettle   undo

dis- is most commonly used to make negative verbs:

disembark   disagree

dis- can also be used in adjectives and nouns:

discontent   discord

mis- can be used to form negative nouns or verbs:

misfortune   misrepresent

ir- is most often used with words that begin with r:

irresponsible   irregular   irradiate

il- is most often used with words that begin with l:

illegal   illegible

im- is used with words that begin with b, m, p:

imbalance   immature   improper

in- can be used with almost any letter:

inability   indefinite   insane

RULE 2: The prefix *for-* means "away, apart, against, off"; *fore-* means "in, at the front of, in advance of."

forbid   foretell

RULE 3: The prefix *dis-* has several forms:

dis- becomes di- before the letters b, d, g, l, m, n, r, v:

diverge   dilute

dis- sometimes becomes dif- before the letter f:

diffuse

dis- (*di-*, *dif-*) has the following meanings when used to create verbs:

dismiss—"away or apart"   disbar—"deprive of or expel from" disfigure—"make the opposite of"   disjoin—"reverse the action of"

disappear, disallow—"fail, cease, refuse to"

dis- also means "not, the opposite of" when used to form adjectives:
dishonest

dis- also means "the opposite of" or "lack of" when used to form nouns:
disunion   disease

RULE 4: The prefix *de-* has some of the same meanings as *dis-*:

derail—"away or apart from, off"   decede—"reverse the action of"

RULE 5: The prefix *pre-* means "before."

premix   prejudge

RULE 6: The prefix *re-* means "do again, repeat."

reread   reconsider

RULE 7: The prefix *en-* means "put, go into or onto; in, within."

enlist

RULE 8: The prefix *co-* means "with, together, joint, jointly."

cooperate

RULE 9: The prefix *uni-* means "one, single."

unisex

C. Rules for Modifying Base Words When Spelling Derived Forms

Note: *In the case of a rare exception, develop mental orthographic images (MOIs) for correct spelling of word.*

RULE 1: In general, drop the final *e* when adding a suffix that begins with a vowel unless the final *e* is needed to condition the final consonant of the base word; do not drop the final *e* when adding a suffix that begins with a consonant. There are a few exceptions to this rule that will require development of MOIs.

notice → noticeable   advise → advisement

RULE 2: For words ending in *y* preceded by a consonant, change *y* to *i* before adding suffixes, unless adding *-y* and *-ness* to one-syllable words.

beauty → beautiful   busy → business   crazy → crazily

shy → shyly   dry → dryness

RULE 3: For words ending in *y* preceded by a vowel, the *y* does not change when suffixes are added.

buy → buyer   convey → conveyance

portray → portrayal

RULE 4: For words ending in *le*, change the *e* to *i* before adding *-fy* to change adjective forms into verb forms.

ample → amplify   example → exemplify

RULE 5: For words ending in *te, ce*, drop the *e* and add *i* before adding *-ous* and *-al* to condition the last consonant segment of the base in the derived form.

commerce → commercial   expedite → expeditious

RULE 6: For words ending in *ce*, drop the *e* and before adding *-tion* to form noun forms.

introduce → introduction   deduce → deduction

RULE 7: For words ending in *de*, change the *de* to *s* before adding *-ion, -ive* to change verb forms into adjective forms.

exclude → exclusion   preclude → preclusive

RULE 8: For words ending in *d* preceded by a consonant, change the *d* to *s* or *t* before adding *-ion* to change verb forms into noun forms.

attend → attention   suspend → suspension

RULE 9: For words ending in *t* proceeded by a vowel, change the *t* to *ss* before adding *-ion* to form noun forms or *-ive* to form adjective forms.

submit → submission   admit → admissive

RULE 10: For words ending in *t* preceded by a consonant, drop the *t* before adding *-cy, -ce* to change noun and adjective forms into noun forms.

agent → agency   reticent → reticence

RULE 11: For words ending in a single consonant *l*, double the *l* before adding *-ent, -ant* to change verb forms into adjective and noun forms.

repel → repellent   propel → propellant

RULE 12: For words ending in *be*, drop the *e* and change *b* to *p* before adding *-tion* to form noun forms.

subscribe → subscription   describe → description

Sample Letter to Parents

Spelling Performance Evaluation for Language and Literacy

Student: Hillary Roberts   Date of Birth: 2/14/1990
School: Dawson School   Date of Test: 6/11/2002
Grade: 6   Age: 12 years, 4 month
Level of SPELL Administered: Level 3   Examiner: Ellen Kraus

Dear Parent,

I used SPELL: Spelling Performance Evaluation for Language and Literacy, to measure Hillary's spelling skills. SPELL is a computer software program that assesses spelling skills and helps determine what type of spelling instruction is needed to improve spelling skills.

Spelling is a complex language and cognition skill that relies on a number of different types of abilities and knowledge. These include:

- **Awareness of speech sounds (Phonological Awareness)** – the ability to think about the individual sounds that make up a word.

- **Knowledge of English phonics and spelling rules or patterns (Orthographic Knowledge)** – the knowledge of and ability to use letters to represent the sounds in a word and to use rules to spell words that follow spelling patterns (for example, silent 'e' at the end of a word to spell long vowel words).

- **Knowledge of word meaning and relationships (Morphological Knowledge and Semantic Relationships)** – the knowledge of and ability to use word meaning to spell certain word suffixes (such as "walk<u>s</u>, walk<u>ing</u>, walk<u>ed</u>") and certain word prefixes (such as "<u>dis</u>continue" and "<u>il</u>legal"); the knowledge of and ability to use familiar, related words to spell more complex words (for example, using "magic" to help spell "magician").

- **Memory for word images (Mental Orthographic Images)** – the ability to store and recall specific visual images of known words.

All of these factors are important for spelling, and each affects how well a student spells. When a student struggles with how to spell words correctly, other aspects of his or her writing, such as grammar, organization and clarity, may be compromised. In addition, improvement in spelling skills has been shown to improve reading skills.

SPELL required Hillary to spell a set of words and possibly to complete a series of additional tasks that provided further information about her spelling. SPELL indicates that Hillary needs to do the following to improve her spelling skills:

SPELL *Letter to Parents*   p. 1 of 2   © 2002 Learning by Design Inc.

112

Roberts, Hillary

1. Awareness of speech sounds (Phonological Awareness)

➢ Hillary needs phonology-based spelling instruction to improve her spelling of:
  ▪ Short Vowel: i / I /

2. Knowledge of English phonics and spelling rules or patterns (Orthographic Knowledge)

➢ Hillary needs phonics-based spelling instruction to improve her spelling of:
  ▪ Unstressed Vowels (Schwas): Schwa in 2 Syllable Words
  ▪ Unstressed Vowels (Schwas): Schwa in 3 Syllable Words
➢ Hillary needs rule- and pattern-based spelling instruction to improve her spelling of:
  ▪ Long Vowel: u spelled as 'ue, oo, o, ui'

3. Knowledge of word meaning and relationships (Semantics and Morphological Knowledge)

➢ Hillary needs semantics and morphology-based spelling instruction to improve her spelling of:
  ▪ Inflected Words: With 'ed, ing' Following Short Vowel
  ▪ Inflected Words: With 'ed, ing' Following Long Vowel
  ▪ Inflected Words: With 's, es" for Plural or Third Person Singular
➢ Hillary needs semantics and morphology-based spelling instruction combined with development of clear and complete mental word images to improve spelling of:
  ▪ Inflected Words: With 'ed, ing' Following Long Vowel
  ▪ Inflected Words: With 's, es" for Plural or Third Person Singular

4. Memory for word images (Mental Orthographic Images)

➢ Hillary needs to develop clear and complete word images to improve her spelling of:
  ▪ Long Vowel: a spelled as 'ey, ay, ai'
  ▪ Other Vowels: Diphthongs 'oy, oi, au'
  ▪ Vocalic 'r, l': Vocalic 'r' spelled as 'er, ir, ur, ear, our, or'
  ▪ Vocalic 'r, l': Vocalic 'l' spelled as 'el, al, le'
  ▪ Unstressed Vowels (Schwas): In 2 syllable words
  ▪ Unstressed Vowels (Schwas): In 3 syllable words
  ▪ Silent 'e' and Silent Consonants: Non-Conditioning Silent 'e' and Silent Consonants

If specific instructional help is needed, I can provide Hillary's classroom teacher with a list of specific suggestions to help Hillary improve her spelling skills. Please let me know if you have any questions about the information in this report.

Thank you,

Ellen Kraus

Ellen Kraus

Sample Letter to Teachers

Spelling Performance Evaluation for Language and Literacy

Student: Hillary Roberts
School: Dawson School
Grade: 6
Level of SPELL Administered: Level 3

Date of Birth: 2/14/1990
Date of Test: 6/11/2002
Age: 12 years, 4 month
Examiner: Ellen Kraus

Dear Teacher,

Hillary was administered SPELL: Spelling Performance Evaluation for Language and Literacy, a computer software assessment tool designed to assess your student's spelling skills. This letter provides information about how Hillary's spelling skills were assessed; the results of this assessment, and, where appropriate, recommendations for ways to improve spelling skills.

Spelling is a complex language and cognition skill that relies on a number of different types of abilities and knowledge. These include:

- **Awareness of speech sounds (Phonological Awareness)** – the ability to think about the individual sounds that make up a word.

- **Knowledge of English phonics and spelling rules or patterns (Orthographic Knowledge)** – the knowledge of and ability to use letters to represent the sounds in a word and to use rules to spell words that follow spelling patterns (for example, silent 'e' at the end of a word to spell long vowel words).

- **Knowledge of word meaning and relationships (Morphological Knowledge and Semantic Relationships)** – the knowledge of and ability to use word meaning to spell certain word suffixes (such as "walk<u>s</u>, walk<u>ing</u>, walk<u>ed</u>") and certain word prefixes (such as "<u>dis</u>continue" and "<u>il</u>legal"); the knowledge of and ability to use familiar, related words to spell more complex words (for example, using "magic" to help spell "magician").

- **Memory for word images (Mental Orthographic Images)** – the ability to store and recall specific visual images of known words.

All of these factors are important for spelling, and each affects how well a student spells. When a student struggles with how to spell words correctly, other aspects of his or her writing, such as grammar, organization and clarity, may be compromised. In addition, improvement in spelling skills has been shown to improve reading skills.

Roberts, Hillary

SPELL required Hillary to spell a set of words and possibly to complete a series of additional tasks that provided further information about her spelling. SPELL indicates that Hillary needs to do the following to improve her spelling skills:

1. **Awareness of speech sounds (Phonological Awareness - PA)**

    ➢ Hillary needs phonology-based spelling instruction to improve her spelling of:
       ▪ Short Vowel: i / I /

2. **Knowledge of English phonics and spelling rules or patterns (Orthographic Knowledge)**

    ➢ Hillary needs phonics-based spelling instruction to improve her spelling of:
       ▪ Unstressed Vowels (Schwas): Schwa in 2 Syllable Words
       ▪ Unstressed Vowels (Schwas): Schwa in 3 Syllable Words
    ➢ Hillary needs rule- and pattern-based spelling instruction to improve her spelling of:
       ▪ Long Vowel: u spelled as 'ue, oo, o, ui'

3. **Knowledge of word meaning and relationships (Semantics and Morphological Knowledge)**

    ➢ Hillary needs semantics and morphology-based spelling instruction to improve her spelling of:
       ▪ Inflected Words: With 'ed, ing' Following Short Vowel
       ▪ Inflected Words: With 'ed, ing' Following Long Vowel
       ▪ Inflected Words: With 's, es" for Plural or Third Person Singular
    ➢ Hillary needs semantics and morphology-based spelling instruction combined with development of clear and complete mental word images to improve spelling of:
       ▪ Inflected Words: With 'ed, ing' Following Long Vowel
       ▪ Inflected Words: With 's, es" for Plural or Third Person Singular

4. **Memory for word images (Mental Orthographic Images)**

    ➢ Hillary needs to develop clear and complete word images to improve her spelling of:
       ▪ Long Vowel: a spelled as 'ey, ay, ai'
       ▪ Other Vowels: Diphthongs 'oy, oi, au'
       ▪ Vocalic 'r, l': Vocalic 'r' spelled as 'er, ir, ur, ear, our, or'
       ▪ Vocalic 'r, l': Vocalic 'l' spelled as 'el, al, le'
       ▪ Unstressed Vowels (Schwas): In 2 syllable words
       ▪ Unstressed Vowels (Schwas): In 3 syllable words
       ▪ Silent 'e' and Silent Consonants: Non-Conditioning Silent 'e' and Silent Consonants

I am including a list of suggestions for implementing these recommendations into your language arts curriculum. I hope you will find this information helpful.

Thank you,

Ellen Kraus

Ellen Kraus

List of Selector Module Test Items

Item #	Word	Sentence
1	boat	I rode the boat across the lake.
2	cane	The man walked with a cane.
3	ear	I hear with my ear.
4	keep	I can keep a secret.
5	kick	I kick a ball with my foot.
6	lung	The lung is a part of our body.
7	match	Use a match to start the fire.
8	ship	A ship is a very big boat.
9	tune	I will sing a tune.
10	honey	The bees make honey.
11	dress	The girl is wearing a dress.
12	fight	The man got hurt in a fight.
13	house	I live in a house.
14	nurse	I went to the nurse when I was sick.
15	cast	The doctor put a cast on my broken arm.
16	sound	The alarm made a loud sound.
17	bottle	The baby drinks from a bottle.
18	bowl	We eat cereal from a bowl.
19	comb	I comb my hair.
20	pause	The teacher asked us to pause for a break.
21	caught	The police caught the robber.
22	cries	The baby cries when he is hungry.
23	stopped	We stopped at the light.

24	babies	The babies are asleep in the cradle.
25	below	My feet are below my knees.
26	biting	She is biting her nails.
27	poison	Poison is very dangerous.
28	repair	He will repair the broken toy.
29	continue	She will continue the story later.
30	skeleton	A skeleton has many bones.
31	magician	The magician did tricks.
32	signal	Give a signal with your hand before you turn.
33	description	I gave a very detailed description to the policeman.
34	lawyer	My sister is a lawyer.
35	extension	The extension cord was not long enough.
36	sailor	A sailor lives on a navy ship.
37	location	The location for practice was changed.
38	eruption	The eruption from the volcano was very large.
39	prisoner	The prisoner escaped from jail.
40	argument	We disagreed and had an argument.

List of Level 1 Main Test Module Items

Item #	Word	Sentence
1	catch	I can catch a ball.
2	boat	I rode the boat across the lake.
3	when	We eat when we are hungry.
4	chain	The chain fell off my bike.
5	key	I lost the key for my house.
6	mood	He is in a good mood.
7	nine	Nine comes before ten.
8	rich	People with a lot of money are rich.
9	tune	I will sing a tune.
10	wacky	This cartoon is wacky.
11	thing	I don't know what this thing is.
12	shop	We shop at a store.
13	head	I wear a hat on my head.
14	jog	We jog for exercise.
15	gum	I like bubble gum.
16	joke	We laughed at his joke.
17	hen	We saw a chicken and a hen at the farm.
18	tie	I will tie my shoes.
19	chase	The dog will chase the cat.
20	coal	Coal is black.
21	fish	Fish swim in water.
22	shock	I got an electric shock.
23	noon	We eat lunch at noon.

24	chip	She has a chip in her tooth.
25	shut	Please shut the door.
26	hope	I hope to see you soon.
27	ear	I hear with my ear.
28	wheel	I broke the wheel on my bike.
29	rule	Always follow the golden rule.
30	jet	We flew on a jet.
31	take	Please take out the garbage.
32	chair	You sit on a chair.
33	kick	I kick a ball with my foot.
34	thief	The thief stole the money.
35	kite	The kite flew high in the sky.
36	chief	We met the fire chief at the station.
37	thick	The opposite of thin is thick.
38	match	Use a match to start the fire.
39	coat	We wear a coat when it is cold.
40	bath	She took a bubble bath.
41	they	They want to go with us.
42	hang	He will hang his clothes in the closet.
43	white	The color of snow is white.
44	touch	I can touch my toes with my fingers.

Continued on next page

Appendix I—*Continued*

45	rake	We must rake the leaves.
46	hide	They like to play hide and seek.
47	cure	There is no cure for a cold.
48	soap	We wash our hands with soap and water.
49	honey	The bees make honey.
50	fail	She does not want to fail the test.
51	food	We eat food when we are hungry.
52	goal	The hockey player scored a goal.
53	sock	I wear a sock on my foot.
54	leaf	The leaf fell from the tree.
55	fire	The fire was burning.
56	moon	We can see the moon at night.
57	hot	The summer is very hot.
58	lung	The lung is a part of our body.
59	why	Please explain why you did this.
60	bus	Children ride to school on a bus.
61	ship	A ship is a very big boat.
62	bake	I will bake some cookies.
63	pie	We eat apple pie.
64	code	We have a secret code.
65	choke	Don't choke on your food.
66	cute	The baby is very cute.
67	job	I work very hard at my job.
68	seal	We saw a seal at the zoo.
69	cane	The man walked with a cane.
70	then	The girl read the book and then put it away.

71	cat	The dog chased the cat.
72	my	This is my friend.
73	wing	The bird has a broken wing.
74	nail	He hit the nail with the hammer.
75	reach	I can't reach the top.
76	sing	She will sing a song.
77	whale	A whale lives in the ocean.
78	shy	The shy girl is very quiet.
79	pool	We swim in a pool.
80	jug	There is water in the jug.
81	rude	He was very rude to me.
82	note	She wrote a note to her mother.

List of Level 2 Main Test Module Items

Item #	Word	Sentence
1	obey	We must obey the law.
2	knife	You cut with a knife.
3	kiss	Grandma gave me a kiss.
4	huge	The size of a dinosaur is huge.
5	switch	She flipped the light switch.
6	kneel	People kneel when they pray.
7	hang	He will hang his clothes in the closet.
8	bunny	The bunny ate a carrot.
9	bottle	The baby drinks from a bottle.
10	why	Please explain why you did this.
11	juice	I like orange juice.
12	those	Those shoes belong to my sister.
13	argue	Please don't argue with me.
14	church	Some people go to church on Sunday.
15	comb	I comb my hair.
16	place	I won first place.
17	dream	I had a bad dream last night.
18	fight	The man got hurt in a fight.
19	black	Black is a dark color.
20	snail	The snail is very slow.
21	calf	The baby calf is eating the grass.
22	page	Turn to the next page

23	rice	We ate rice and beans.
24	guilt	The judge will determine the man's innocence or guilt.
25	though	He can go though I don't think he will.
26	ruby	She wore ruby slippers.
27	catch	I can catch a ball.
28	bass	We caught a bass fish.
29	final	He gave his final answer.
30	cry	I cry when I am sad.
31	think	I think I should go home now.
32	state	California is a state.
33	pause	The teacher asked us to pause for a break.
34	rifle	He used a rifle to go hunting.
35	sleep	We sleep during the night.
36	shock	I got an electric shock.
37	cider	I like to drink apple cider.
38	thing	I don't know what this thing is.
39	boss	I have a nice boss at work.
40	ladder	I climbed up the ladder.
41	cold	It is cold in winter.
42	traffic	We got stuck in heavy traffic.
43	knock	They heard a knock on the door.
44	gentle	The girl was gentle with the puppy.
45	dress	The girl is wearing a dress.
46	when	We eat when we are hungry.
47	motor	The car motor would not start.
48	goose	I saw a goose by the pond.

Continued on next page

Appendix J—*Continued*

49	her	Her name is Nicole.
50	wrong	The boy gave the wrong answer.
51	city	New York is a city.
52	they	They want to go with us.
53	pink	The doll's dress was pink.
54	treat	I gave my dog a treat.
55	goal	The hockey player scored a goal.
56	rake	We must rake the leaves.
57	jeep	We drove in the jeep.
58	wrist	I fell down and broke my wrist.
59	niece	I played with my nephew and niece.
60	smoke	We saw smoke from a fire.
61	flush	You flush a toilet.
62	table	Please set the table.
63	cure	There is no cure for a cold.
64	plank	The pirate walked the plank.
65	oil	They drill for oil.
66	wild	Squirrels are wild animals.
67	loyal	A loyal friend is a true friend.
68	cost	The book cost a lot of money.
69	chair	You sit on a chair.
70	throat	She has a sore throat.
71	super	The teacher said I did a super job.
72	house	I live in a house.
73	raid	The army will raid the enemy camp.
74	wheel	I broke the wheel on my bike.

75	spider	The spider made a web.
76	wrestle	The boys will wrestle on the mat.
77	thumb	We have one thumb on each hand.
78	hold	Please hold my hand.
79	rule	Always follow the golden rule.
80	scissors	She cut the paper with scissors.
81	truck	They took the boxes off the truck.
82	shop	We shop at a store.
83	ruler	We measured the distance with a ruler.
84	limb	They cut a limb off the tree.
85	bush	The rabbit is under the bush.
86	champ	He is the football champ.
87	white	The color of snow is white.
88	brick	The house is made of brick.
89	penny	She put the penny in her purse.
90	choke	Don't choke on your food.
91	brave	The soldier was very brave.
92	myself	I completed the work by myself.
93	wing	The bird has a broken wing.
94	note	She wrote a note to her mother.
95	cast	The doctor put a cast on my broken arm.
96	true	The answer is true or false.
97	beard	The man shaved his beard.
98	nurse	I went to the nurse when I was sick.
99	later	I will see you later.
100	rich	People with a lot of money are rich.

Continued on next page

Appendix J—*Continued*

101	nice	My teacher is very nice.
102	bowl	We eat cereal from a bowl.
103	germ	A germ can make you sick.
104	cook	I will cook dinner tonight.
105	happy	I am happy to see my friend.
106	vapor	Try not to inhale the vapor.
107	long	The movie was very long.
108	bruise	He has a black and blue bruise from falling down.
109	humor	He has a good sense of humor.
110	code	We have a secret code.
111	squirt	We filled the squirt gun with water.
112	half	I will share half of the cookie.
113	sour	Lemons taste sour.
114	joy	Our new baby fills my life with joy.
115	center	Your nose is in the center of your face.
116	sound	The alarm made a loud sound.
117	shut	Please shut the door.
118	fruit	An apple is a fruit.
119	please	Please do me a favor.
120	room	Please clean up your room.
121	yellow	Yellow is the color of the sun.
122	gem	The gem sparkled in the light.
123	law	You should obey the law.
124	whale	A whale lives in the ocean.
125	bright	The sun is very bright.
126	tool	She used a tool to fix the toy.

127	blue	Blue is a color.
128	staple	She will staple the papers.
129	baby	The baby is in the stroller.
130	rattle	The baby dropped her rattle.
131	cute	The baby is very cute.
132	hammer	We need a hammer and nails.
133	scrabble	I like to play Scrabble.
134	match	Use a match to start the fire.
135	flute	I play the flute in the band.
136	camel	The camel lives in the desert.
137	joke	We laughed at his joke.
138	bomb	The bomb exploded.
139	chain	The chain fell off my bike.
140	job	I work very hard at my job.
141	unite	Let's unite together.

List of Level 3 Main Test Module Test Items

Item #	Word	Sentence
1	loyal	A loyal friend is a true friend.
2	wild	Squirrels are wild animals.
3	squirt	We filled the squirt gun with water.
4	cause	The rain will cause a flood.
5	scrabble	I like to play Scrabble.
6	poison	Poison is very dangerous.
7	wrong	The boy gave the wrong answer.
8	switch	She flipped the light switch.
9	knocked	Someone knocked on the door.
10	whisker	The cat lost a whisker.
11	correct	The answer is correct.
12	ancient	We study ancient history.
13	jungle	Lions live in the jungle.
14	giraffe	The giraffe has a very long neck.
15	black	Black is a dark color.
16	champ	He is the football champ.
17	mouth	Close your mouth when you chew.
18	putting	I am putting the dishes away.
19	argued	The boys argued about who should go first.
20	pennies	Five pennies equal one nickel.
21	wheels	A car has four wheels.
22	smoke	We saw smoke from a fire.
23	chains	We use chains to lock our bikes.

24	behind	They hid behind the wall.
25	babies	The babies are asleep in the cradle.
26	escape	The prisoner will try to escape.
27	speech	The winner gave a speech.
28	though	He can go though I don't think he will.
29	hopping	The rabbit is hopping.
30	calves	The two baby calves are eating grass.
31	joy	Our new baby fills my life with joy.
32	bunny	The bunny ate a carrot.
33	sipped	She sipped the iced tea.
34	built	They built a large fence.
35	fruit	An apple is a fruit.
36	below	My feet are below my knees.
37	hoping	He is hoping for a raise.
38	ladder	I climbed up the ladder.
39	huge	The size of a dinosaur is huge.
40	avoid	He is trying to avoid me.
41	remote	We are going to a remote island.
42	funeral	The funeral will be at the cemetery.
43	chore	He has one more chore to finish.
44	comb	I comb my hair.
45	holds	A glass holds water.
46	true	The answer is true or false.
47	why	Please explain why you did this.
48	churches	People pray in churches.
49	violent	The war movie was violent.

Continued on next page

129

Appendix K—*Continued*

50	unit	An inch is a unit of measure.
51	vapor	Try not to inhale the vapor.
52	bussed	The children were bussed to school.
53	benefit	Everyone will benefit from the donation.
54	stopped	We stopped at the light.
55	burns	Wood burns in a fire.
56	pages	We read 50 pages of the book.
57	excuse	Please excuse me.
58	whales	Whales swim in the ocean.
59	puppets	We made puppets for the show.
60	vitamin	Take a vitamin every day.
61	thumbs	I have two thumbs.
62	circle	A circle is round.
63	pedals	A bike has two pedals.
64	office	She works in an office building.
65	houses	People live in houses.
66	found	We found some money on the sidewalk.
67	super	The teacher said I did a super job.
68	rule	Always follow the golden rule.
69	hated	They hated the music.
70	smash	I saw him smash the pumpkin.
71	despite	She went out with no jacket despite the cold.
72	seated	We were seated in the first row.
73	halves	She gave me both halves of the cookie.
74	baby	The baby is in the stroller.
75	caught	The police caught the robber.

76	wrestled	He wrestled the man to the ground.
77	yellow	Yellow is the color of the sun.
78	swing	You push a swing.
79	direct	The police officer will direct the traffic.
80	skeleton	A skeleton has many bones.
81	whisper	Please whisper when you are in the library.
82	sound	The alarm made a loud sound.
83	they	They want to go with us.
84	germ	A germ can make you sick.
85	shutting	He is shutting the door.
86	bottle	The baby drinks from a bottle.
87	bushes	The rabbits are under the bushes.
88	myself	I completed the work by myself.
89	getting	I am getting hungry.
90	mistake	The girl was careful not to make a mistake.
91	music	We listen to music.
92	secret	I heard a secret.
93	flush	You flush a toilet.
94	snake	A snake crawls on the ground.
95	repair	He will repair the broken toy.
96	roped	The police roped off the crime scene.
97	chips	Please pass the potato chips.
98	those	Those shoes belong to my sister.
99	ribbons	The package is tied with ribbons.
100	singing	They are singing a song.
101	explore	They will explore the woods.

Continued on next page

131

Appendix K—*Continued*

102	manage	I can manage the work by myself.
103	spoon	We eat ice cream with a spoon.
104	fighting	She is fighting with her brother.
105	bucket	Fill the bucket with water.
106	polite	The nice boy is so polite.
107	fueled	The mechanic fueled the airplane before takeoff.
108	batting	He is batting the ball.
109	filed	I filed the papers in a folder.
110	obeys	A good person obeys the law.
111	throat	She has a sore throat.
112	goose	I saw a goose by the pond.
113	beard	The man shaved his beard.
114	padded	Football players wear padded uniforms.
115	define	We use a dictionary to define a word.
116	locate	I cannot locate the building.
117	joked	He joked around and made everyone laugh.
118	thinking	She is thinking of an answer.
119	center	Your nose is in the center of your face.
120	lights	She turned on the lights.
121	deleting	I am deleting my old files.
122	snail	The snail is very slow.
123	knife	You cut with a knife.
124	cries	The baby cries when he is hungry.
125	rattle	The baby dropped her rattle.
126	milking	The farmer is milking the cow.
127	whips	The horseman used two whips.

128	sighed	We sighed in relief when we heard the news.
129	hanging	They are hanging pictures on the wall.
130	gem	The gem sparkled in the light.
131	socket	Put the plug into the socket.
132	tomorrow	Tomorrow is another day.
133	paint	The man will paint a picture.
134	nice	My teacher is very nice.
135	attitude	The girl has a bad attitude.
136	watched	We watched TV last night.
137	humor	He has a good sense of humor.
138	because	I eat because I am hungry.
139	produce	They will produce their work by the end of the week.
140	cider	I like to drink apple cider.
141	even	A number is odd or even.
142	jolly	We had a jolly good time.
143	kittens	The cat has seven kittens.
144	being	It is fun being a circus clown.
145	usual	I ordered my usual drink.
146	things	I don't know what those things are.
147	happy	I am happy to see my friend.
148	kept	They kept the dog in the house.
149	long	The movie was very long.
150	bored	We were bored and fell asleep.
151	table	Please set the table.
152	bright	The sun is very bright.
153	camel	The camel lives in the desert.

Continued on next page

133

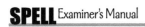

Appendix K—*Continued*

154	catches	He catches a ball.
155	flake	A flake of snow landed on my nose.
156	spider	The spider made a web.
157	heard	I heard a secret.
158	shopping	The man is shopping for food.
159	hold	Please hold my hand.
160	continue	She will continue the story later.
161	juices	Juices are made from fruit.
162	stretch	I need to stretch my legs.
163	paid	We paid the bill before we left.
164	channel	I want to change the channel.
165	city	New York is a city.
166	science	I studied for my science test.
167	alone	I don't like to be home alone.
168	combed	She combed her hair.
169	keys	I lost the keys to my house.
170	fever	She is sick with a fever.
171	truck	They took the boxes off the truck.
172	cure	There is no cure for a cold.
173	rice	We ate rice and beans.
174	jabbed	She jabbed me with her pencil.
175	shock	I got an electric shock.
176	leaves	He raked all the leaves in the yard.
177	agree	We agree to play by the rules.
178	deserve	I deserve to be paid for my work.
179	loaves	He bought two loaves of bread.

List of Level 4 Main Test Module Test Items

Item #	Word	Sentence
1	kept	They kept the dog in the house.
2	whisks	He whisks the eggs with a fork.
3	paid	We paid the bill before we left.
4	halves	She gave me both halves of the cookie.
5	appealing	The scholarship offer I received is very appealing.
6	juices	Juices are made from fruit.
7	hated	They hated the music.
8	whistling	He is whistling a tune.
9	pennies	Five pennies equal one nickel.
10	attitude	The girl has a bad attitude.
11	argued	The boys argued about who should go first.
12	cries	The baby cries when he is hungry.
13	scratching	The dog is scratching his neck.
14	chimneys	Black smoke came out of both chimneys.
15	thrown	The ball was thrown by the pitcher.
16	babies	The babies are asleep in the cradle.
17	attached	A copy of the answer sheet was attached.
18	calves	The two baby calves are eating grass.
19	office	She works in an office building.
20	leaves	He raked all the leaves in the yard.
21	switch	She flipped the light switch.
22	refuse	I refuse to tell a lie.

Continued on next page

Appendix L—*Continued*

23	goose	A saw a goose by the pond.
24	local	We belong to the local swim club.
25	continuous	The band played continuous music.
26	chapter	I finished reading the last chapter in the book.
27	description	I gave a very detailed description to the policeman.
28	bottle	The baby drinks from a bottle.
29	fueled	The mechanic fueled the airplane before takeoff.
30	fruit	An apple is a fruit.
31	excuse	Please excuse me.
32	sensible	She is a very sensible person.
33	importance	The importance of the tie-breaking game made him nervous.
34	illegal	Illegal drugs can be very dangerous.
35	remote	We are going to a remote island.
36	spray	I got wet from the spray of water.
37	explore	They will explore the woods.
38	mouth	Close your mouth when you chew.
39	though	He can go though I don't think he will.
40	vapor	Try not to inhale the vapor.
41	jolly	We had a jolly good time.
42	manager	He is the store manager.
43	wrong	The boy gave the wrong answer.
44	hanging	They are hanging pictures on the wall.
45	busily	The students busily completed their work.
46	revisit	I want to revisit Europe someday.
47	brightness	The brightness of the sun hurt my eyes.
48	humor	He has a good sense of humor.

49	resignation	They announced his resignation at work today.
50	scissors	She cut the paper with scissors.
51	excellent	She wrote an excellent report.
52	sailor	A sailor lives on a navy ship.
53	mistake	The girl was careful not to make a mistake.
54	germ	A germ can make you sick.
55	argument	We disagreed and had an argument.
56	commercial	The TV commercial was fun to watch.
57	despite	She went out with no jacket despite the cold.
58	homeless	The homeless man was looking for a job.
59	meteor	We watched the meteor shoot across the sky.
60	model	The model posed for a picture.
61	ladder	I climbed up the ladder.
62	partisan	He is a Republican partisan.
63	simple	This math problem is very simple.
64	polite	The nice boy is so polite.
65	extension	The extension cord was not long enough.
66	hobbies	I enjoy many hobbies.
67	define	We use a dictionary to define a word.
68	wrestled	He wrestled the man to the ground.
69	deleting	I am deleting my old files.
70	choice	He made a choice about which project to do first.
71	pleasure	It's a pleasure to meet you.
72	fright	Scary movies cause fright in some young children.
73	escape	The prisoner will try to escape.
74	yearn	I yearn to go on vacation.

Continued on next page

Appendix L—*Continued*

75	ethical	He demonstrated ethical behavior in his work.
76	snake	A snake crawls on the ground.
77	blouses	The girls wore two different blouses.
78	coexist	We must learn to coexist peacefully.
79	simplify	She asked her teacher to simplify the directions.
80	knives	Both knives were very sharp.
81	jury	The judge asked the jury for their decision.
82	jungle	Lions live in the jungle.
83	eruption	The eruption from the volcano was very large.
84	turtle	A turtle moves slowly.
85	shady	They sat under the shady tree.
86	spark	A spark from the fire burned my hand.
87	spruce	A spruce tree is in our yard.
88	criticize	We should not criticize someone's mistakes.
89	whales	Whales swim in the ocean.
90	signal	Give a signal with your hand before you turn.
91	slimy	A worm feels slimy.
92	knocked	Someone knocked on the door.
93	feminist	A feminist supports women's rights.
94	waiter	The waiter brought our food.
95	cautious	Be very cautious with matches.
96	circle	A circle is round.
97	legality	He questioned the legality of the action.
98	those	Those shoes belong to my sister.
99	pushy	Some salespeople are very pushy.
100	misinterpret	I hope he does not misinterpret what I said.

101	dictionary	I checked the spelling of the word in the dictionary.
102	title	The book has an interesting title.
103	spry	The dancer's movements were spry.
104	edition	I bought the new edition of the book.
105	quickly	He quickly did his work.
106	unusual	The behavior was unusual for him.
107	heard	I heard a secret.
108	citizen	The citizen is proud of his city.
109	promptness	The boss recognized my promptness in completing my work.
110	enable	This ticket will enable you to get into the show.
111	hesitant	The boy was hesitant to cross the street.
112	magician	The magician did tricks.
113	yellow	Yellow is the color of the sun.
114	penniless	He lost his job and is penniless.
115	wonderful	She is a wonderful person.
116	empower	A good manager will empower his employees.
117	below	My feet are below my knees.
118	dependent	A young child is dependent upon his parents.
119	whips	The horseman used two whips.
120	disciplinary	The boy received disciplinary action for fighting at school.
121	swinging	The children are swinging on the swings.
122	digestible	It's good to eat food that is easily digestible.
123	fierce	The fierce winds did a lot of damage.
124	funeral	The funeral will be at the cemetery.
125	banged	I banged my toe on the chair.
126	production	The production was delayed.

Continued on next page

Appendix L—*Continued*

127	catches	He catches a ball.
128	likeable	My friends are very likeable.
129	fever	She is sick with a fever.
130	huge	The size of a dinosaur is huge.
131	slice	She offered me a slice of bread.
132	disregard	Some drivers disregard stop signs.
133	socket	Put the plug into the socket.
134	noticeable	The scratch is noticeable.
135	violence	The violence grew out of control.
136	permissive	I'm glad the school policy is permissive of casual dress.
137	commendation	The fireman received a commendation for his brave work.
138	black	Black is a dark color.
139	built	They built a large fence.
140	myself	I completed the work by myself.
141	legalize	The law was changed to legalize concealed weapons.
142	silliness	They laughed at the silliness of the story.
143	speech	The winner gave a speech.
144	persistence	Her persistence got her what she wanted.
145	smoke	We saw smoke from a fire.
146	disagree	I disagree with your answer.
147	slightly	One is slightly larger than the other.
148	punishable	The crime is punishable by law.
149	irrational	His irrational behavior was difficult to manage.
150	journalist	My father is a journalist for the local newspaper.
151	changeable	The weather can be very changeable.
152	competency	She demonstrated her competency for the job.

153	skating	I enjoy skating in the winter.
154	incorrect	Her answer was incorrect.
155	swing	You push a swing.
156	whisker	The cat lost a whisker.
157	brainy	He is a brainy student.
158	bored	We were bored and fell asleep.
159	residential	We live in a residential part of the city.
160	caught	The police caught the robber.
161	exclusive	He was accepted to an exclusive school.
162	cause	The rain will cause a flood.
163	expeditious	He shipped the package the most expeditious way.
164	recollect	I cannot recollect what she said.
165	strain	I saw a doctor about the strain in my back.
166	predetermine	They could not predetermine how much the repairs would cost.
167	soothing	The music is very soothing.
168	continuity	There is continuity in the series of books she wrote.
169	permission	She gave us permission to go.
170	responsible	I am responsible for my behavior.
171	found	We found some money on the sidewalk.
172	shovel	We removed the snow with a shovel.
173	tomorrow	Tomorrow is another day.
174	channel	I want to change the channel.
175	buckle	She asked us to buckle our seat belts.
176	poisonous	Snakebites can be poisonous.
177	unicycle	The clown rode on a unicycle.
178	flush	You flush a toilet.

Continued on next page

Appendix L—*Continued*

179	bomb	The bomb exploded.
180	joked	He joked around and made everyone laugh.
181	loaves	He bought two loaves of bread.
182	batting	He is batting the ball.
183	bussed	The children were bussed to school.
184	padded	Football players wear padded uniforms.

Glossary

ABUTTING CONSONANTS: Adjacent consonants that do not form a blend (e.g., *ct* in *correct).*

ACTIVE ATTENTION: A focused effort to the task at hand.

AFFRICATES: Consonant speech sounds produced as a stop before a fricative: /ʧ/ and /ʤ/.

ALLOPHONE: A phonetic (sound) change in the pronunciation of a phoneme that does not change the meaning of a word (e.g., /pʰɪg/ for /pɪg/).

ALPHABETIC PRINCIPLE: The use of letters and letter combinations to represent sounds.

ALVEOLAR FLAP: The reduction of a medial /t/ or /d/ to a less distinctive sound when it occurs between an accented (stressed) and unaccented (unstressed) syllable (e.g., *letter, writer, model, ladder).*

BASE WORD: A free morpheme; a word that can stand alone and has meaning without a prefix or a suffix (e.g., *dig).*

CONSONANT BLEND: A combination of two or three adjacent consonants (sounds or letters) within the same syllable and in which each letter is pronounced (e.g., *bl* in *blue* or *str* in *street);* this term is used interchangeably with *consonant cluster.*

BOUND MORPHEME: A morpheme that has meaning only in combination with another morpheme (e.g., bat*s).*

CONSONANT CLUSTER: See CONSONANT BLEND.

CONDITIONING SILENT *E:* A silent *e* that causes the preceding consonant to be a soft consonant (i.e., pronounced as a fricative or an affricate; e.g., *lace, page).*

CONDITIONING VOWEL: Any vowel that causes the preceding consonant to be a soft consonant (i.e., pronounced as a fricative or an affricate; e.g., *lace, page, edition, intelligible).*

CONSONANT: A phoneme that is not a vowel and is formed with the obstruction of air between the lips, teeth, or tongue, with the manner and place of the restriction determining the particular consonant production.

CONSONANT DIGRAPH: Two graphemes pronounced as one phoneme (e.g., *sh* = /ʃ/ and *th* = /θ/ or /ð/).

CONTINUANTS: Consonant speech sounds that can be spoken continuously until the speaker runs out of breath, (e.g., /s, m, v/); all English phonemes except the stops (i.e., except /p, t, k, b, d, g/).

DERIVATIONAL MARKER: A prefix or suffix that when added to a root or a base word changes the meaning and/or the word class (e.g., *teach + er = teacher* and *un + fair = unfair).*

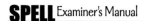

DERIVED FORM: A word containing a derivational marker (e.g., invest*ment);* also called *derived word.*

DIPHTHONG: A vowel speech sound composed of two adjacent vowels in the same syllable pronounced as a gliding from one sound to another but still producing only one phoneme: /ɑɪ, ɔɪ, ɑʊ/.

DISTINCTIVE FEATURES: The distinguishing characteristics of speech sounds.

FREE MORPHEME: A morpheme that can stand alone (i.e., that has meaning without combination with another morpheme; e.g., *bat).*

FRICATIVES: Consonant speech sounds spoken with significant obstruction to a continuous airflow: /s, z, ʃ, ʒ, f, v, θ, ð, h/.

GRAPHEME: A letter in the written form.

GLIDES: Consonant speech sounds that glide into the following vowel: /w, j, hʷ/.

INFLECTED FORM: A word containing an inflectional marker (e.g., walk*ed);* also called *inflected word.*

INFLECTIONAL MARKER: A bound morpheme that when added to a base word provides information about time or quantity without changing the word class (e.g., *walk + ed = walked* and *cat + s = cats).*

IRREGULAR PAST TENSE: A past tense verb that does not follow conventional spelling rules (e.g., *caught).*

LAX VOWELS: Vowels that are pronounced without tension and with shorter duration than long vowels; vowel sounds that do not have a relationship to the letter or letter name; include the five common lax vowel sounds most commonly associated with short vowels *a, e, i, o, u* and also include the vowel /ʊ/ as in *book* and the vowel /ɔ/ as in *bought.*

LIQUID CLUSTER: A combination of two or three adjacent consonants within the same syllable and including an *l* or *r* (e.g., *flake, produce).*

LIQUIDS: Consonant speech sounds spoken with a minimal amount of obstruction of airflow by the tongue: /l, r/.

MENTAL ORTHOGRAPHIC IMAGE: The specific visual representation of a known word in the mental lexicon (i.e., long-term memory storage of a word).

LONG VOWEL: A vowel that is pronounced with tension and with longer duration than short vowels; as used by educators, a vowel that is pronounced as its letter name: *a, e, i, o, u.*

METACOGNITIVE: The conscious awareness of thinking about one's own thinking processes.

MINIMAL PAIRS: A pair of words that differ in only one phoneme (e.g., *pen, pin).*

MORPHEME: A unit of semantic meaning (e.g., *bats* contains two morphemes: *bat* and *s).*

MORPHOLOGICAL AWARENESS: Metalinguistic awareness of the semantically meaningful units of words.

MORPHOLOGICAL KNOWLEDGE: Explicit information about the morphology of a language.

MORPHOLOGY: The study of the structure of the meaningful units in words and how they are combined to form words.

NASALS: Consonant speech sounds spoken with airflow directed through the nasal cavity: /m, n, ŋ/.

NASAL CLUSTER: A combination of two or three adjacent consonants within the same syllable and including *m, n,* or *ng* (e.g., cha*mp*, behi*nd*, thinki*ng).*

NONCONDITIONING SILENT *E:* A silent *e* that does not affect the pronunciation of the preceding consonant (e.g., lik*e*, cap*e).*

OPAQUE DERIVATION: The process that results in a derived word that is marked by both a phonemic (or allophonic) change in the base portion of the word and the full spelling of the base word is not contained within the derived form (e.g., *busy* ➔ *busily, admit* ➔ *admission).*

ORTHOGRAPHIC KNOWLEDGE: Explicit information about sound symbol correspondences, letter patterns, and positional and phonetic constraints on letter patterns.

ORTHOGRAPHIC TRANSPARENCY: The orthography of the base word remains intact in the derived form (i.e., the full spelling of the base word can be seen within the derived form; e.g., *poisonous, charger, magician).*

ORTHOGRAPHY: The writing system of a language.

ORTHOTACTIC PRINCIPLES: Rules of a writing system that dictate positional constraints. (e.g., *ng* is not used at the beginning of English words or the digraph *ck* is only used in the middle or end of English words).

OTHER VOWEL: A term used for lax vowels other than the five common lax vowel sounds most commonly associated with the short vowels *a, e, i, o, u;* includes the vowel /ʊ/ as in *book* and the vowel /ɔ/ as in *bought.*

OVERGENERALIZATION: The process of applying a linguistic rule or pattern beyond its intended use without regard for the meaning (e.g., *trust* spelled as *trussed).*

PATTERNS AND RULES: Similarities among items that can be used to group them; when items are grouped, students should be able to describe the "rule" for an item belonging to the group.

PHONEME SEGMENTATION: The metalinguistic ability to separate a word into individual phonemes (e.g., *cat* has three phonemes: /k, æ, t/.

PHONEMES: The smallest meaningful unit of speech that combines with other sounds to form words.

PHONEMIC AWARENESS: The metalinguistic awareness that words consist of individual sounds and that these sounds in words can be manipulated.

PHONEMIC DISCRIMINATION: The metalinguistic ability to discern the subtle differences between phonemes that signal changes in meaning.

PHONETIC: Properties of sounds that do not signal changes in meaning.

PHONICS: The study of the relationships between letters and the sounds they represent.

PHONOLOGICAL AWARENESS: The metalinguistic awareness of all aspects of the phonological structure of language from individual phonemes to syllable structure, word boundaries, and prosody.

PHONOLOGICAL TRANSPARENCY: A characteristic whereby the phonology of a base word remains intact in its derived form (e.g., *penniless)*; includes allophonic change if allophones occur in free variation in production of the base word.

PHONOLOGY: The study of the sound system of language and the rules that govern those sounds.

PLURAL: A morpheme that signifies more than one (e.g., bat*s*).

PREFIX: A morpheme that precedes a root or a base word or another prefix and that modifies the meaning of the base word (e.g., *un*happy).

ROOT WORD: A morpheme that can stand alone and to which prefixes and suffixes may be added.

S- CLUSTERS: A combination of two or three adjacent consonants within the same syllable and including an *s* (e.g., *sw-* or *str-).*

SCHWA: A nondistinct vowel in unstressed syllables (e.g., *about).*

SELF-DISCOVERY: Learning situations that may be orchestrated and facilitated by an instructor that allow for the student to glean a rule or pattern (e.g., sorting activities in which the rule to fit into a category must be discovered and stated by the student).

SELF-REGULATION: The act of using strategies such as self-talk, planning, and monitoring actions to assist in the accomplishment of a goal.

SEMANTICS: The study of the meanings of words.

SHORT VOWEL: A term used by educators to refer to the five lax vowel sounds most commonly associated with the short vowels *a, e, i, o, u.*

SIBILANTS: Consonant speech sounds that are spoken with high frequency noise, or a "hissing" sound: /s, z, ʃ, ʒ, ʧ, ʤ/.

SONORANTS: Speech sounds that are spoken with minimal obstruction of the airflow; includes vowels, glides, liquids, and nasals.

SOUND-SYMBOL CORRESPONDENCE: The relationship between a single sound or phoneme and the letter(s) or grapheme(s) that represent the sound.

STOPS: Consonant speech sounds that are spoken with complete blocking of the air stream: /p, b, t, d, k, g/; also called *plosives*.

STRESSED SYLLABLE: An accented syllable in which the vowel sound is distinct.

SUFFIX: A morpheme that follows a root or a base word or another suffix and that modifies the meaning of the base word (e.g., advis*or)*.

SYLLABLE SEGMENTATION: The meta-linguistic ability to separate a word into individual syllables (e.g., *pencil* has two syllables: *pen* and *cil)*.

SOCIAL-CONSTRUCTIVIST THEORY: The theory that learning occurs in a social context and is enhanced through the instructor providing specific support for the learner's attempts at learning new material.

THIRD PERSON PRESENT TENSE: A verb containing the inflectional markers *-s* or *-es* (e.g., *walks, washes)*.

TRANSPARENCY: A characteristic of derived words whereby the phonology and/or the orthography of the base word remains intact in the derived form.

UNSTRESSED SYLLABLE: An unaccented syllable in which the vowel sound is minimized and nondistinct.

VISUAL ORIENTATION: The direction of letters (e.g., *b* and *d* have the reverse visual orientation).

VOCALIC *R:* The syllabic /ɝ/ or /ɚ/ sound, as in *germ* and *actor*.

VOCALIC *L:* The syllabic /l/ sound, as in *candle* and *legal*.

Helpful Resources

ⓖeneral/Theoretical

American Speech-Language-Hearing Association. (2001). *Roles and responsibilities of speech-language pathologists with respect to reading and writing in children and adolescents: Position statement, guidelines, and technical report*. Rockville, MD: Author.

Apel, K. (1999). Checks and balances: Keeping the science in our profession. *Language, Speech, and Hearing Services in Schools, 30,* 98–107.

Bear, D., Invernizzi, M., Templeton, S., & Johnston, F. (2000). *Words their way: Word study for phonics, vocabulary, and spelling instruction* (2nd ed.). Upper Saddle River, NJ: Prentice Hall.

Blachman, B. (1994). What we have learned from longitudinal studies of phonological processing and reading, and some unanswered questions: A response to Torgesen, Wagner, and Rashotte. *Journal of Learning Disabilities, 27,* 287–291.

Bruck, M., & Waters, G. (1988). An analysis of the spelling errors of children who differ in their reading and spelling skills. *Applied Psycholinguistics, 9,* 77–92.

Carlisle, J. F., & Nomanbhoy, D. M. (1993). Phonological and morphological awareness in first graders. *Applied Psycholinguistics, 14,* 177–195.

Catts, H. W., & Kamhi, A. G. (Eds.). (1999). *Language and reading disabilities*. Needham Heights, MA: Allyn & Bacon.

Edwards, H. T. (1992). *Applied phonetics: The sounds of American English*. Singular: San Diego, CA.

Ehri, L. C. (1998). Grapheme-phoneme knowledge is essential for learning to read words in English. In J. L. Metsala and L. C. Ehri (Eds.), *Word recognition in beginning literacy* (pp. 3–40). Mahwah, NJ: Erlbaum.

Ehri, L. C. (1998). Word reading by sight and by analogy in beginning readers. In C. Hulme and R. M. Joshi (Eds.), *Reading and spelling: Development and disorders* (pp. 87–112). Mahwah, NJ: Erlbaum.

Hewitt, L. E. (2000). Does it matter what your client thinks? The role of theory in intervention: Response to Kamhi. *Language, Speech, and Hearing Services in Schools, 31,* 186–193.

Lennox, C., & Siegel, L. S. (1996). The development of phonological rules and visual strategies in average and poor spellers. *Journal of Experimental Psychology, 62,* 60–83.

Logemann, J. A. (2000). From the president: Are clinicians and researchers different? *The ASHA Leader, 5*(8), 2.

Lyon, G. R., & Moats, L. C. (1997). Critical conceptual and methodological considerations in reading intervention research. *Journal of Learning Disabilities, 30,* 578–588.

McGuinness, D. (1997). Decoding strategies as predictors of reading skill: A follow-on study. *Annals of Dyslexia, 47,* 117–150.

Mersand, J., Griffith, F., & Griffith, K. (1996). *Spelling: The easy way* (3rd ed.). Hauppauge, NY: Barron's Educational Series.

Moats, L. (2000). *Speech to print: Language essentials for teachers.* Baltimore: Brooks.

Muter, V. (1998). Phonological awareness: Its nature and its influence over early literacy development. In C. Hulme & R. M. Joshi (Eds.), *Reading and spelling: Development and disorders* (pp. 113–126). Mahwah, NJ: Erlbaum.

National Institute of Child Health and Human Development. (2000). *Report of the national reading panel: An evidence-based assessment of the scientific research literature on reading and its implications for reading instruction.* Bethesda, MD: NICHD Clearinghouse.

Nunes, T., Bryant, P., & Bindman, M. (1997). Learning to spell regular and irregular verbs. *Reading and Writing: An Interdisciplinary Journal, 9,* 427–449.

Nunes, T., Bryant, P., & Bindman, M. (1997). Morphological spelling strategies: Developmental stages and processes. *Developmental Psychology, 33,* 637–649.

Swank, L. K., & Catts, H. W. (1994). Phonological awareness and written word decoding. *Language, Speech, and Hearing Services in Schools, 25,* 9–14.

Treiman, R. (1998). Why spelling? The benefits of incorporating spelling into beginning reading instruction. In J. L. Metsala & L. C. Ehri (Eds.), *Word recognition in beginning literacy* (pp. 289–314). Mahwah, NJ: Erlbaum.

Vaughn, S., Schumm, J. S., & Gordon, J. (1993). Which motoric condition is most effective for teaching spelling to students with and without learning disabilities? *Journal of Learning Disabilities, 26,* 191–198.

Venezky, R. L. (1999). *The American way of spelling.* New York: Guilford Press.

Worthy, J., & Viise, N. M. (1996). Morphological, phonological, and orthographic differences between the spelling of normally achieving children and basic literacy adults. *Reading and Writing: An Interdisciplinary Journal, 8,* 139–159.

ssessment/Intervention

Apel, K., & Masterson, J. J. (2001). Theory-guided spelling assessment & intervention: A case study. *Language, Speech, and Hearing Services in Schools, 32,* 182–195.

Apel, K., & Masterson, J. J. (1997). Child language-learning disorders. In T. A. Crowe (Ed.), *Applications of counseling in speech-language pathology and audiology* (pp. 220–237). Baltimore: Williams and Wilkins.

Apel, K., & Swank, L. K. (1999). Second chances: Improving decoding skills in the older student. *Language, Speech, and Hearing Services in Schools, 30,* 231–242.

Berninger, V. W. (1999). Coordinating transcription and text generation in working memory during composing: Automatic and constructive processes. *Learning Disabilities Quarterly, 22,* 99–112.

Berninger, V. W., Vaughan, K., Abbott, R. D., Brooks, A., Abbott, S. P., Rogan, L., Reed, E., & Graham, S. (1998). Early intervention for spelling problems: Teaching functional spelling units of varying size with a multiple-connections framework. *Journal of Educational Psychology, 90,* 587–605.

Blachman, B., Ball, E., Black, R., & Tangel, D. (1994). Kindergarten teachers develop phoneme awareness in low-income, inner-city classrooms. *Reading and Writing: An Interdisciplinary Journal, 6,* 1–18.

Cunningham, P. M. (1998). The multisyllabic word dilemma: Helping students build meaning, spell, and read "big" words. *Reading and Writing Quarterly: Overcoming Learning Difficulties, 14,* 189–218.

Gillon, G. T. (2000). The efficacy of phonological awareness intervention for children with spoken language impairment. *Language, Speech, and Hearing Services in Schools, 31,* 126–141.

Graham, S., & Harris, K. R. (1999). Assessment and intervention in overcoming writing difficulties: An illustration from the self-regulated strategy development model. *Language, Speech, and Hearing Services in Schools, 30,* 255–264.

Henderson, E. (1990). *Teaching spelling.* Boston: Houghton Mifflin.

Mersand, J., Griffith, F., & Griffith, K. O. (1996). *Spelling the easy way* (3rd ed.). Hauppauge, NY: Barron's Educational Series.

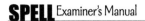

Moats, L. (1994). Assessment of spelling in learning disabilities research. In G. R. Lyon (Ed.), *Frames of reference for the assessment of learning disabilities* (pp. 333–350). Baltimore: Brookes.

Pressley, M., Wharton-McDonald, R., & Mistretta, J. (1998). Effective beginning literacy instruction: Dialectical, scaffolded, and contextualized. In J. L. Metsala and L. C. Ehri (Eds.), *Word recognition in beginning literacy* (pp. 357–374). Mahwah, NJ: Erlbaum.

Scott, C. M. (2000). Principles and methods of spelling instruction: Applications for poor spellers. *Topics in Language Disorders, 20*(3), 66–82.

Seiger, B. (1985). *Mastering spelling*. Englewood, NJ: Prentice Hall Regents.

Singer, B. D., & Bashir, A. S. (1999). What are executive functions and self-regulation and what do they have to do with language-learning disorders? *Language, Speech, and Hearing Services in Schools, 30*, 265–273.

Yopp, H. K. (1995). A test for assessing phonemic awareness in young children. *The Reading Teacher, 49*, 20–29.

References

Beggs, A., Schofield, E., Masterson, J., & Apel, K. (2001, November). *Differences in spelling accuracy between handwritten and keyboard response modalities*. Poster session presented at the annual convention of the American Speech-Language-Hearing Association, New Orleans, LA.

Carlisle, J. F. (1995). Morphological awareness and early reading achievement. In L. B. Feldman (Ed.), *Morphological aspects of language processing* (pp. 189–209). Hillsdale, NJ: Erlbaum.

Derwing, B. L., Smith, M. L., & Wiebe, G. E. (1995). On the role of spelling in morpheme recognition: Experimental studies with children and adults. In L. B. Feldman (Ed.), *Morphological aspects of language processing* (pp. 189–209). Hillsdale, NJ: Erlbaum.

Ehri, L. C. (2000). Learning to read and learning to spell: Two sides of a coin. *Topics in Language Disorders, 20*(3), 19–36.

Ehri, L., & Wilce, L. (1982). Recognition of spellings printed in lower and mixed case: Evidence for orthographic images. *Journal of Reading Behavior, 14,* 219–230.

Fowler, A. E., & Lieberman, I. Y. (1995). The role of phonology and orthography in morphological awareness. In L. B. Feldman (Ed.), *Morphological aspects of language processing* (pp. 189–209). Hillsdale, NJ: Erlbaum.

Glenn, P., & Hurley, S. (1993). Preventing spelling disabilities. *Child Language Teaching and Therapy, 9,* 1–12.

Larsen, S. C., Hammill, D. D., & Moats, L. C. (1999). *Test of Written Spelling–4*. Austin, TX: Pro-Ed.

Masterson, J. J., & Apel, K., (2000). Spelling assessment: Charting a path to optimal intervention. *Topics in Language Disorders, 20*(3), 50–65.

Masterson, J. J., & Crede, L. A. (1999). Learning to spell: Implications for assessment and intervention. *Language, Speech, and Hearing Services in Schools, 30,* 243–254.

Nation, K., & Hulme, C. (1997). Phonemic segmentation, not onset-rime segmentation, predicts early reading and spelling skills. *Reading Research Quarterly, 32,* 154–167.

Treiman, R., & Bourassa, D. C. (2000). The development of spelling skills. *Topics in Language Disorders, 20*(3), 1–18.

Treiman, R., Cassar, M., & Zukowski, A. (1994). What types of linguistic information do children use in spelling? The case of flaps. *Child Development, 65,* 1310–1329.